First published as a Fireside Book
an imprint of
Simon & Schuster, Inc.
New York 1985

Revised edition published in the United Kingdom by
David & Peta Moeller 1994

ISBN 07111 0060 8

Printed and bound in Great Britain by
BPC Paperbacks Ltd
A member of
The British Printing Company Ltd

WIN THE LOTTERY!

HOW TO PICK YOUR PERSONAL LUCKY NUMBERS

By

ELLIN DODGE

CONTENTS

To Dad with love

... with thank yous to Skipper who helped make
writing this book lle-zy.

INTRODUCTION

Winning the lottery will be a "Love Boat" to freedom. With the help of your predictable lucky numbers the gangplank will come down and you step aboard. The lucky numbers will book your luxury suite.

Personal numbers describe character and personality, your lifetime opportunities and your destiny. When you adopt personal numbers you can link a **chosen first name** and an **individual birthdate** for either yourself or for each of your loved ones. Numerology symbolizes the connection between *your* name, *your* time, *your* life path and *your* destination. It indicates the path to the "the good life" for you and your family.

This system can be applied anytime you want an adventure - anytime you want to have a flutter and play with numbers. There are sets of personal lucky numbers for all in the family. The generation gap closes when the family plays its numbers. Together you can plot the numbers, plan your dream trips and travel in style. The system is a guide to forecast sunny weather and the stormy days since personal lucky numbers will combine with the universal calendar in the lottery life.

When playing the lottery or when you're deciding to buy a home or business, the numbers that you select have cyclic frequencies that accept or reject you. Your personal numbers send out frequencies too, like the waves of the ocean, ebbing and flowing in predictable cycles. These waves are converted to a personal numbers system called numerology.

Numbers have vibrations, explanations and magnetism. The simple arithmetic technique of ancient numerology identifies the number symbols that have undercurrents pulsating for you. By using numerology to chart the vibrations of your name and birthday, you discover your consistent cycles and their mystical number representatives. You can use these numbers to increase your ability to attract the same numbers.

When taking part in a billion pound lottery where the stakes are high, it's reassuring to have a system, to have an edge on the odds - to find the numbers that are attracted to us - to know the numbers that are destined to bring us good fortune?

You may notice that certain numbers seem to surface in your daily routine. You may sense that they belong to you. Lucky or unfortunate, they follow wherever you go. You discover your special numbers by noticing that they appear in addresses, phone numbers or vehicle licence plates: it's a "hit or miss" observation. You usually remember them after they bob up - after they occur - after they have created a lifetime of luxury cruises for someone else.

November 25 1943 **Paul Burnett**   (14) (5) (4) (17) (8) (28) (?)

Why not promenade on the deck of the good ship **Numerology**? You'll find her ready to sail to Shangri-la and the Fortunate Isles that encircle Psychic Whoopeeland. Welcome aboard!

TIMING YOUR FLUTTER

Your numbers are primed to pop up in the lottery when your number vibrations are mixed with the number cycles of the calendar day. When the vibrations are mingled, you synchronize yourself to the universal trends. Your energy reaches out to grab the opportunity of the moment. When opportunity and timing are matched, winners are born. You can lend yourself a hand up the ladder of success by tuning to the number frequency governing universal energy every day. This knowledge taps you into cosmic consciousness.

HOW DO YOU KNOW WHEN YOU ARE LUCKY?

Numbers accompany your moves from place to place. They show themselves whenever your energy is very high or very low. Extremes of emotional activity heighten your transmitting power. Emotional reactions alter your physical chemistry, which starts a chain reaction to charge and enlarge your magnetic fields. If you accept the concept that there is an electricity in numbers and that they have a relationship to one another, you can understand how numbers attract or repel one another. The trick is to find your frequency and meet the dynamics of the universal calendar. When you lock into perfect timing, you cuddle up to Dame Fortune.

It is at these times, when you connect with the universal calendar, that Lady Luck rides on your shoulder: you are ripe to play and chance your arm. The calendar date numbers are intertwined with your destiny. When your name and birthday numbers are compatible with the calendar numbers, it's time to have a flutter.

USE THE VIBES

I'll bet that you've sensed that numbers have vibrations. But even if you haven't, you probably have heard people say that dice have vibes, rooms have vibes and people have vibes. In Las Vegas and Monte Carlo, the clockless casinos have a wall of timeless energy that you can cut with a knife. Who needs to know what time it is. You pick up the vibes and allow free drinks and deep-piled carpets to set the stage.

But it's difficult to be a winner standing next to someone with opposite goals. It's better to have supportive people around. Their energy boosts yours because they probably have the same or complementary numbers that mingle with yours. When you're

January 6 1956 **Angus Deayton**   (17)(8)(1)(26)(10)(9)(?)

involved in a game of chance, even if it's an occasional pastime, you are a player for that moment, steeped in optimism, intuition and superstition.

PROTECT YOUR ENERGY SPACE

Negative thoughts, the close proximity of opposite magnetism, or people concentrating their energy on numbers that challenge your personality or destiny numbers reach into your space. They are using their opposing energy to sap yours. They have the unconscious desire to alter or close channels to anyone's intuitional feelings except their own. When the vibes in my surroundings are shattered, I know it. I expect that you know the feeling too.

The positive energy you need for playing a game of chance drains when opposites are near. They interrupt the concentration and visualization needed to bring your numbers up. Be aware that you should remove yourself, break the energy and leave discord behind. You can, and should, purchase your lottery tickets on a day when you're free of opposition. When in doubt, don't play.

You can alter the vibes by changing the timing of your entries or buying a lottery ticket on a different day. A sensitive pontoon player will walk around, observe the action, and move on to play at a different table. As a numerology-smart lottery player you can avoid

playing in the presence of non-supportive people, or
when you sense that your energy is off-key.

CHIME TO YOUR OWN TUNE

We have a tempo to our lives. Numerology describes the progressions we experience through
number symbols. In the symphony of life, we are
tuned, unconsciously and numerologically, to
respond to our own music. We attract people and
experiences that have the same numbers. These
numbers show up in people's names, birthdates,
house addresses, phone numbers, and even social
security numbers. It's true, in a practical sense, that
social security numbers are spewed indiscriminately
from a computer. However, in the teachings of the
ancients, it is said that "there are no accidents" - no
coincidences - and we attract what "is meant to be."
It's a matter of deciding whether we will be "open"
or "closed" to a consciousness that uses the sensing
mind - not the physical brain.

THE NUMBERS SYSTEM

Numerology, a numbers system that began with the
cave peoples, is known to stem from ancient Egypt,
is included in the Indian VEDAS, the Chinese CIRCLE
OF THE HEAVENS, the Hebrew KABALA, and was
part of the Phoenician and Chaldean cultures. It is
still a useful tool today. Numerology was refined by

April 3 1924 **Marlon Brando**   (28)(1)(2)(23)(5)(20)(?)

the ancient Greeks and, in its updated system, makes it possible for you to discover the magnetic and mystical medley of numbers that corresponds to your personality and destiny.

Numerology's system for personal lucky numbers is based upon the numbers that correspond with the letters in your first name. A simple reduction of the name numbers is used to create an inverted pyramid that gives you the root number of your name. The inverted pyramid is called the ABRACADABRA. The numbers of your month, day and year are used to find your destiny. An interaction of birthdate numbers is used to find your age category and the best lucky number for the present time. The calendar day lucky number - a mix of month, day and year - is used with your name and birthdate numbers when playing the lottery.

By mixing the numerics of the universe with your personal number symbols you engage the energy coming from the media, the population as a whole, and the activity of the lottery organization. Your concentrated power means that you may be singing numerology's praises all the way to the bank. By using numerology to find your personal lucky numbers, and co-ordinating your actions to the tempo of the universal calendar numbers, you're likely to hang a framed gold record in the music room of your mediterranean villa. However, to go for the gold, it helps to have a direct route - a system.

January 26 1925 **Paul Newman**   (14)(5)(4)(44)(8)(18)(?)

YA GOTTA HAVE FAITH

Even when you're tuned to your personal numerology numbers your chemistry changes at the precise moment you buy your lottery ticket. The moment you mark your cards you're intensifying and electrifying your numbers. Your universal frequency is charged; you and the lottery find a common ground. Faith is a grand partner and your belief in your *system* opens a direct line to Lady Luck.

You are playing with millions of people who are emotionally stimulated. Everyone's talking about the fabulous financial prize for a winner. Communication sends out super electronic waves. It is the unique excitement that sparks your special numbers to seek their counterparts on those little balls in the lottery birdcage.

The atmosphere is charged and intensified by enthusiasm, impulsiveness and a spirit of adventure. All you have to do is to concentrate on your numbers and to co-ordinate your lucky numbers with the calendar days that correspond.

Backing yourself - investing in your own talents will give you better odds.

This system reveals the secret of lost civilizations by explaining that numbers have a rapport and gravitate to themselves. Correlations have existed through the ages, and coincidence after coincidence has pointed

---

June 25 1963 **George Michael**   (39) (3) (6) (14) (5) (31) (?)

to the truth that "like attracts like". Opposites may attract at first blush, but before they establish a rapport, sparks fly, and the connection is momentarily severed. To win the lottery, the impression of your vibrations should not be broken. Your ability to visualize yourself receiving the money and hearing yourself accept the congratulations of others is an energy booster.

PARA-SCIENCE???

Astrology, numerology's sister in the structuring of coincidence, describes character and forecasts experiences by time, date and place of birth - feats studied through the movement of planets. Astrology cannot tie in your number co-ordinates but, coincidentally, was proven to be accurate long before computerized techniques revealed that people born at the same time and place have common traits. There is no scientific proof to support its accuracy - but the beliefs linger in the daily astrology newspaper columns that are read by millions before they scan the front-page news of the day.

Numerology traces its origins to cavemen, who related emotionally to their experiences. If they built a good fire with four pieces of wood, the number four became a symbol for something dependable and constructive. All numbers have double meanings, based upon experiences like these. Far from being coincidence number meanings stem from fact. Superstition is no more than coincidences observed and applied to down-to-earth realities through the ages. The supermundane happenings of intuition and coincidence go hand in hand. Numerology puts you in touch with a *numbers system* that has the uncanny ability to find your frequency in the universal scope of coincidence.

The organized structure used in this book and the theory that numbers are attractive to themselves was defined by Pythagoras - father of geometry, teacher of astronomy and founder of the diatonic scale (laws of musical progression by which we still tune our pianos today). In the sixth century B.C., at his university-temple in Greece, his disciples followed him in a religion he based on interpretations of the cosmic vibrations that he measured as they emanated from the spheres. He gave the number symbols for one (1) through nine (9) human personality, character, talents and life experience meanings. He would have agreed with Bo Derek, that ten (10) is perfect.

These numbers, in Pythagoras's system, describe the steps that lead - when applied to name letters - to a perfection of character and wisdom. But the number ten (10) is never interpreted as perfection in Psychic Whoopeeland. It is considered to be on another plane of existence and therefore, as we live a practical life with inevitable compromises, perfection is unobtainable.

July 18 1950 **Richard Branson** (43) (7) (8) (40) (4) (33) (?)

PLAYING YOUR PERSONAL NUMBERS

When the numbers within the birthdate are interpreted, they describe life experiences that the person born on that day will meet.

It is this factor in the numerology system that provides the additional push to bring a punter close to perfection - to a 'win' position. The lottery draws upon the energies of today. The punter and the magnetic forces described by numbers can be synchronized. The relationship of your destiny to the activities in focus for the calendar day are revealed by the simple arithmetic of numerology. This book provides you with the key for entering the lottery. Drawing calendar dates that relate to your destiny - your lucky days will meet with your lucky numbers. It's the day that the numbers are drawn - not the day you purchase your ticket - that is important.

THE NUMBERS SYSTEM

Five numbers that are personal to you plus the calendar day number form the basis for the six-number WIN THE LOTTERY! system. In the following pages, you will learn to calculate your personal numbers. Your first name as it appears on your birth certificate, and your birthdate, as it appears on your birth certificate, are used in the ABRACADABRA name pyramid and the birthday classic pyramid. The system for finding the calendar day number is based upon the current month, day and year that the lottery numbers are drawn.

USING THE LUCKY NUMBERS WHEEL

You have your five **base** personal lucky numbers. If two or more are the same number, you do have alternatives. Any number, double or single, may be "wheeled" in to a harmonious lucky number. For example, Michelle Pfeiffer has the numbers 1(37, 3 + 7 = 10, 1 + 0 = 1), 1, 10, 1, 51. She needs to wheel the number 1 twice without using No.10 which would also be a wheeled number of no.1! She must also replace number 51 because the Lottery is chosen from 1 to 49.

She will choose 37(her natural unreduced first name number), 1 (her natural root number), 19(her birthday number 1 wheeled to 19), 10(her natural reduced destiny number) and 6 (her pyramid numbers, reduced to a single number 6). Michelle's resulting personal lucky numbers will be, 37 : 1 : 19 : 10 : 6. She also has other alternative wheeled numbers, if she wishes, as explained and listed in Chapter VII, but these should be her first choice.

Sally Gunnell also has a similar first name number and ABRACADABRA root number 6. Sally may wheel either of the two numbers to 15, (1 + 5 = 6), 24, (2 + 4 =6), 33,(3 = 3 + 6) or 42, (4 + 2 = 6). Her first choice should be 15 and 6. As Sally is a popular first name Sallys should make a note of these wheeled alternatives.

I have given the five personal base lucky numbers of many celebrity stars on each page with a wheeled number where necessary, to show that everyone has a minimum of five different personal numbers. I have given the natural "first name number"(unreduced) and then the five circled numbers. Note that there are only five. The sixth number is dependent upon the day that the Lottery is drawn.

THE NUMBERS

LUCKY No. 1. The total of the number values of the letters in your first name.

LUCKY No. 2. The root number of the first name ABRACADABRA.

LUCKY No. 3. The total number of your month, day and year of birth.

LUCKY No. 4. The reduced number of the total of your month, day and year of birth.

LUCKY No. 5. The birthday classic pyramid number for your present age category.

LUCKY No. 6. The number of the calendar day the lottery numbers are drawn.

July 29 1966 **Sally Gunnell** (15) ⑥ ⑥ ⑬ ④ ㊱ ⑦

CHAPTER

1

LUCKY No.1

YOU ARE YOUR FIRST NAME

The first choice number is the number total of your first name. The second choice will be your name root number in the ABRACADABRA. Your name is your music, and its vibrations are intensely connected to you. Your talents, personality, self-image, strong and weak points are pulsating within its numbers. Your first name number is your *power number*. You will notice it cropping up in your daily routine. You will find that you choose friends with the same name total or who have a first letter that corresponds to your name total. Where numbers are involved, like attracts like.

People who have the same name have the same numbers and vibrations. However, when you mix your name numbers with your birthdate numbers, you create your own unique chord. When your

April 10 1932 **Omar Sharif**   (20)(2)(3)(29)(11)(19)(?)

chord complements the melody of the calendar day and is in tune with the lottery energy, they attract one another. That's when winners are born.

LUCKY No. 1
HOW TO CREATE YOUR NAME NUMBER
REFER TO THE LETTER VALUES CHART TO FIND THE NUMBER EQUIVALENTS FOR THE LETTERS IN YOUR FIRST NAME.

LETTER-VALUES CHART

1	2	3	4	5	6	7	8	9
A	B	C	D	E	F	G	H	I
J	K	L	M	N	O	P	Q	R
S	T	U	V	W	X	Y	Z	

Step 1.   Print the letters of your first name in the top line of the boxes provided, one letter in each box.

Step 2.   Enter the number equivalent in the box below each letter.

Step 3.   Add the numbers across. Enter the total after the equals sign (=) at the end of the line. This is your lucky number.

Step 4.   If you end up with a double number, add the two digits to reduce it to a single number. Enter the single reduced number in the second "total" box.

Step 5.   This is your name number.

= □ = □ = □

Example: *Jonathan*

Step 1.

J	O	N	A	T	H	A	N										

= □ = □

Step 2.

J	O	N	A	T	H	A	N										
1	6	5	1	2	8	1	5										

= □ = □

Step 3.   Lucky Number

J	O	N	A	T	H	A	N										
1	6	5	1	2	8	1	5										

= 29 = □

$1 + 6 + 5 + 1 + 2 + 8 + 1 + 5 = 29$

A DOUBLE NUMBER. REDUCE THE DOUBLE NUMBER TO A SINGLE NUMBER

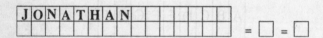

Step 4.

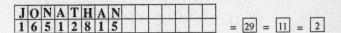

A DOUBLE NUMBER REDUCED TO A SINGLE NUMBER $2 + 9 = 11$, $1 + 1 = 2$

Step 5.   LUCKY No.1. is 2 if your first name is JONATHAN.

Example: *Sam*

Step 1.

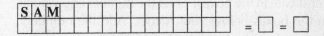

Step 2.

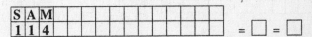

Step 3.

Step 4. $1 + 1 + 4 = 6$ - A SINGLE NUMBER

Step 5.   LUCKY NUMBER 1 is 6 if your first name is SAM.

January 10 1949 **Rod Stewart** (36)(9)(8)(34)(7)(44)(?)

DO IT YOURSELF

LETTER-VALUES CHART

1	2	3	4	5	6	7	8	9
A	B	C	D	E	F	G	H	I
J	K	L	M	N	O	P	Q	R
S	T	U	V	W	X	Y	Z	

Print your first name as it appears on your birth certificate in the boxes. Enter the number equivalents in the boxes below your name. Add the numbers. Reduce to a single number, if necessary.

□□□□□□□□□□□□□□ = □ = □ = □

YOU ARE YOUR FIRST NAME AND YOU ARE WONDERFUL!

Your vibrations are reinforced when you understand yourself. The following abbreviated number definitions will help you to understand the number that you have just found to be the *power number* for your first name.*

May 2 1969   **Brian Lara**   (26)(8)(2)(32)(5)(7)(?)

A NUMBER 1 NAME

Your name is gifted with individualism, creativity and energy to enable you to think progressively for yourself and others. You are best suited to be your own boss and to take the lead inventively. You do not like to be told when or how to get your work done. Negatively - you may be too impatient, changeable and self-centred.

A NUMBER 2 NAME

Your name is gifted with sensitivity to others, a consciousness of detail and ability to carry out instructions. You are best suited to work co-operatively and to be the "glue" that binds families and organizations together. You do not like tactlessness, disharmony or inconsiderate people. Negatively - you may be too shy, modest and careless.

A NUMBER 3 NAME

Your name is gifted with imagination, optimism and sociability. You are best suited to work with people, to be surrounded by beauty and to be self-expressive. Words are your tool. You do not like ugliness, gloom or boredom. Negatively - you may scatter your interests, talk too much or too little, and decline to present a fashionable, cheerful or entertaining facade.

July 28 1936 **Garfield Sobers** (44)(8)(3)(18)(9)(26)(?)

A NUMBER 4 NAME

Your name is gifted with structure, management and common sense. You are best suited to work, systemize, organize and produce a practical result. You do not like disorder, disloyalty or superficiality. Negatively - you may be creatively self-limiting, too rule-bound or a rule-breaker, and use your dedication to get a job done unwisely, as a workaholic does.

A NUMBER 5 NAME

Your name is gifted with youthful enthusiasm, cleverness and versatility. You are best suited to work in a non-routine environment where you are free to use unconventional ideas and your ability to understand people. You do not like to be cloistered, shouted down or locked into traditional-conventional expectations. Negatively - you may be too irresponsible, impulsive and eager to take avocation.

A NUMBER 6 NAME

Your name is gifted with a sense of responsibility, a need to foster harmony or maintain peace, and a strong sense of "right and wrong." You are best suited to work with groups, to uplift or comfort others, and where you are given a position of trust. You do not like to be a loner, to be surrounded by uncaring people or to be impersonal. Negatively - you may volunteer too much, worry needlessly and be too parental.

A NUMBER 7 NAME

Your name is gifted with authority, introspection and a loner's need for privacy. You are best suited to work with your mind - to think, study and investigate. You are secretive and quality conscious. You do not like noisiness, imperfection or crudeness, You have an aristocratic, perfectionist, aloof manner. Negatively - you may be too fault finding, cold and skeptical.

A NUMBER 8 NAME

Your name is gifted with businesslike judgement, thoroughness and executive leadership. You are best suited to be a problem solver. You work for major material results with commercial-financial-worldly projects. You are self-reliant, dependable and mentally alert. You avoid details and delegate responsibility. You do not like to lose control, waste time or become inefficient. Negatively - you may be impatient, intolerant and demanding.

September 5 1940 **Raquel Welch** (29)(2)(8)(28)(10)(23)(?)

A NUMBER 9 NAME

Your name is gifted with empathy, charity and self-lessness. You are best suited to give service to major artistic, communications or humanitarian agencies. You are noble, romantic and magnetic. You attract notables and require a polish and a skill of performance from yourself and others. You do not like bigotry, vulgarity or egocentricity. Negatively - you may be too generous or unforgiving, too emotional or too cold and too petty.

*If you want to know more: Detailed descriptions will be found in YOU ARE YOUR FIRST NAME by Ellin Dodge, a dictionary of over 1,450 names, to be published in the U.K. in the Spring of 1995

May 4 1952 *Michael Barrymore* (33) (6) (9) (26) (8) (30) (?)

CHAPTER

LUCKY No. 2

THE ABRACADABRA - YOUR CHILDHOOD MOTIVATION

The ABRACADABRA is a mystical system. Just as superstitions are not based upon scientific laws of cause and effect, but often are unaccountably accurate, the ABRACADABRA is uncanny. It is that small voice of the child within you, disciplined by life's exposures. Through it, you trace your nurturing environment and your feelings at that time. Use the ABRACADABRA to find the key number at the base of your first name. This key *root number* allows you to understand the character of your introverted self.

The ABRACADABRA *root number* brings the first name to its birthright - back to youth's environmental influences - and provides the key to character formation. Our characters churn with compromises as we grow older.

May 27 1943 ***Cilla Black*** (45) (9) (4) (49) (13) (22) (?)

The attraction that this root number has to itself is vigorous, resounding and omnipotent. It has the intensity to look into the eye of the cyclone and to make a beeline for its counterparts. It is a lifetime weather forecaster and describes the way in which persons bearing the name it signifies cope with experience. How does it work? It works the same way as saying "Gesundheit" ("your health" in German) or "Felicita" ("blessing" or "good luck" in Italian) or "God bless you" in English. It is a good luck omen that wards off negative omens. It is a protective wish word.

CALL IT PSYCHIC WHOOPEE AND LET IT WORK FOR YOU

Secrets have been hidden by priests and the leaders of ancient civilizations throughout the ages. In Helyn Hitchcock's book "Helping Yourself With Numerology", she describes the inverted pyramid or triangle as a magical formula of the ABRACADABRA: "The triangle method had its origin in the great pyramids of Cheops in Gizeh, Egypt, which contains all the secrets of the ages." Ms. Hitchcock describes the system with a base of nine (9) name letters or their equivalent numbers. I have found that the inverted pyramid system is revealing when applied to a first name only.

May 22 1970 **Naomi Campbell** (25) (7) (7) (44) (8) (27) (?)

PUNTERS TAKE ALL THE HELP THEY CAN GET

Psychic Whoopee - the para-sciences, ESP, intuition - whatever you want to call information that we get from the impossible-to-document sources, is unfathomable. Superstition is impossible to explain logically.

Let's face it... when you play you are not being practical. Most people try to believe that "everything comes in threes," "cats have nine lives" or find themselves knocking on wood to avoid bad luck or becoming concerned that breaking a mirror may attract misfortune. If you prefer to sneer at superstition, let me share "The World Book Of Knowledge" explanation. The word means "that which stands above or survives". There are scientists who deny superstitions yet carry a rabbit's foot for good luck. Many play the lottery, are seen in London Casino Clubs and won't step on a crack when they walk down the pavement! People aim for scientific thinking but revert to taking all the help they can get when millions are at stake.

If you think you're using common sense when you have a flutter, you are either a dyed -in - the - wool punter or self-deluding. However, the ABRACAD-ABRA number can be added to your collection of lucky superstitions and can demonstrate your unconscious affinity for Psychic Whoopee.

July 2 1956 **Jerry Hall** (31) (4) (1) (30) (3) (23) (?)

LUCKY No. 2
HOW TO CREATE
YOUR ABRACADABRA NUMBER

LETTER-VALUES CHART

1	2	3	4	5	6	7	8	9
A	B	C	D	E	F	G	H	I
J	K	L	M	N	O	P	Q	R
S	T	U	V	W	X	Y	Z	

Step 1.   Print your first name as it appears on your birth certificate.

Step 2.   Refer to the LETTER-VALUES CHART above. Enter the number equivalent for each letter of your name directly underneath it.

Step 3.   Add the digits across each line by twos. Each line will show one number less than the line above.

RULE FOR ADDING: Reduce all double numbers to single numbers by adding their digits together. Enter

each double number in the upper portion of its box.
Enter each single number in the lower portion of its
box.

Example: 23: 2 + 3 = 5

28: 2 + 8 = 10;

reduce again: 1 + 0 = 1

PANIC NOT! Examples follow

IMPORTANT

Do you now have two
similar personal base
numbers ?

If yes: wheel one of the
numbers!

See Chapter VII

Example: CHARLES
ABRACADABRA

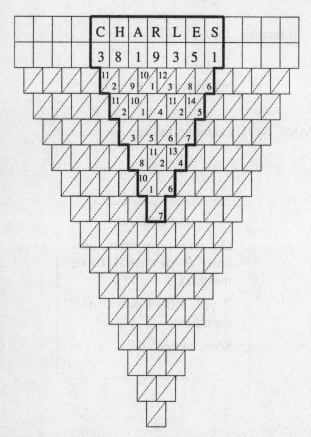

The ABRACADABRA base or *root number* of the name Charles is 7. Charles should play 7.

May 6 1953 **Tony Blair** (34) (7) (6) (29) (11) (24) (?)

Example: DIANA
ABRACADABRA

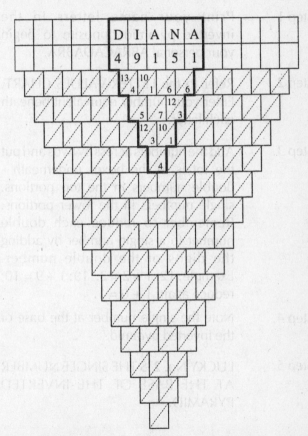

The **ABRACADABRA** base or *root number* of the name DIANA is 4. Diana should play 4.

October 12 1944 **Angela Rippon**   (22) (4) (9) (40) (4) (7) (?)

DO IT YOURSELF

Step 1.   Print your name letters in the inverted pyramid opposite to begin your personal ABRACADABRA.

Step 2.   Refer to the LETTER-VALUES CHART. Enter your number equivalent beneath each letter.

Step 3.   Add the numbers across by twos and put the totals in the boxes underneath - double numbers in the top portions, single numbers in the lower portions. Remember to reduce each double number to a single number by adding the digits of the double number. Example: 12: 1 + 2 = 3. 19: 1 + 9 = 10; reduce again 1 + 0 = 1.

Step 4.   Note the single number at the base of the inverted pyramid.

Step 5.   LUCKY No. 2 IS THE SINGLE NUMBER AT THE BASE OF THE INVERTED PYRAMID.

October 27 1939 **John Cleese**   (20)(2)(3)(14)(5)(32)(?)

ABRACADABRA

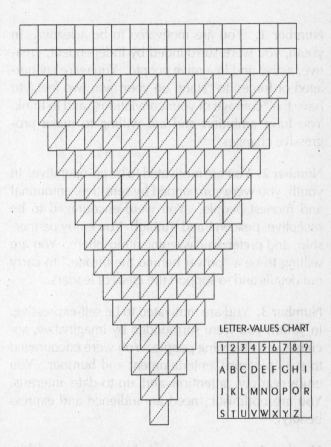

LETTER-VALUES CHART

1	2	3	4	5	6	7	8	9
A	B	C	D	E	F	G	H	I
J	K	L	M	N	O	P	Q	R
S	T	U	V	W	X	Y	Z	

YOUR CHILDHOOD MOTIVATION - ABRACADABRA BASE NUMBER MEANINGS

Number 1. You are motivated to be a leader. In youth, you were surrounded by independent, creative, active and inventive people. You were encouraged or forced to "stand on your own two feet," to have the "courage of your convictions" and to think. You have ambition and are willing to make progressive changes.

Number 2. You are motivated to be co-operative. In youth, you were surrounded by sensitive, emotional and modest people. You were encouraged to be receptive, peaceful and truthful. You enjoy partnership, and prefer an easygoing atmosphere. You are willing to be a "power behind the throne," to carry out details and to support the ideas of leaders.

Number 3. You are motivated to be self-expressive. In youth, you were surrounded by imaginative, sociable and charming people. You were encouraged to seek pleasure, entertainment and humour. You enjoy variety, attention and up-to-date interests. You are optimistic, need an audience and express beauty.

Number 4. You are motivated to be a dependable, managerial worker. In youth, you were surrounded by down-to-earth, traditional, practical people. You were encouraged to be loyal, dedicated and orderly. You enjoy tangible results, building for the future and discipline. You have common sense.

Number 5. You are motivated to be unconventional. In youth, you were surrounded by surprising experiences, non-routine people and you were given the freedom to learn from experience. You were encouraged to experiment, to be adaptable and to show enthusiasm. You enjoy sensuality, travel and freedom. You are clever.

Number 6. You are motivated to be responsible. In youth, you were surrounded by family, took on burdens and became sympathetic and idealistic. You were encouraged to be conventional, to love beauty and to protect others. You enjoy comfort, "roots" and provide domestic or group harmony. You have a listening ear for problems, counsel broadmindedly and volunteer to help.

Number 7. You are motivated to be a perfectionist. In youth, you were surrounded by analytic, introspective, reserved people. You were encouraged to think before you spoke, to respect quality - not quantity - and to know how to keep a secret. You fear loneliness and poverty and guard your emotional reactions. You are aristocratic, prefer not to dirty your hands, and prefer to be aloof from mundane realities.

March 17 1964 **Rob Lowe**   (33)(6)(3)(40)(4)(20)(?)

Number 8. You are motivated to be a material achiever. In youth, you were surrounded by large-minded, strong, dominant people. You were encouraged to be ambitious, to develop stamina and to be confident of your personal courage. You enjoy money, efficiency, and having your work pay off. You are geared to be an executive and have little patience for petty goals or details; you are determined to be successful.

Number 9. You are motivated to be a humanitarian and to serve noble causes. In youth, you were surrounded by philosophical, unselfish and romantic or artistic people. You were encouraged to use your intuition, to be unselfish and to understand emotional and physical suffering. You enjoy being magnetic, being a great lover and inspiring others to do their best. You have a desire to provide and receive a polish and skill of performance. You have the spirit of "brotherly love" and can be heroic.

IMPORTANT

Do you now have two similar personal base numbers ?

If yes: wheel one of the numbers!

See Chapter VII

May 18 1953 **Pierce Brosnan**   (38) (2) (5) (39) (12) (41) (?)

CHAPTER

LUCKY No. 3

YOUR BIRTHDAY NUMBER

"No man is an island".

When you know which oceans you will cross, you can use your sonar to test the depths and forsee the swells. When you keep the horizon in sight, check your charts and prepare for stormy weather, you will be shipshape when you reach your destination. Numerology plots your course and then hands over the tiller. It's your ship. You are the "master of your destiny".

You have responsibility for yourself, your crew and your vessel. If you buck the winds, ignore foghorns in the night, or refuse to plot before you sail, you are bound to meet Father Neptune. If you respect the fickle waters, know maritime law, and have your sea legs planted firmly on the deck, the oceans will take you to explore foreign lands and their unknown customs.

HOW TO SET YOUR COURSE

It is your judgement, the way you cope with the types of people and experiences that you are intended to meet that secures your happiness and material success. Your *destiny number* (your birthday number) explains what you are intended to do and what you will finally become. You usually realize your potential later in life, and you say "If only I was a little bit younger and knew what I know now". Understanding your destiny number will allow you to be in control now instead of later.

If the number of your name is the same as your *destiny number*, you have the talent and personality to meet and greet the people and experiences that cross your path. That's the reason why some children instinctively choose a career and get on with their education or technical experience in their teens. Others must wait and see. They may not enjoy their work until experience teaches them to seek out pleasurable jobs or a late-in-life academic education.

If the number of your name is not the same as your *destiny number*, you will live by the "hunt with the pack" method. You will learn that "experience is the best teacher" and that following your first instinct is the best reward in life. Destiny will call out to you and its soul mates. It echoes, as you repeatedly "turn a deaf ear" to your intuition, turn off at dead-end streets, and pick up troublesome hitchhikers along the route.

CALENDAR POWER

You will taste, touch, smell, see and hear your destiny as you follow your life. You get hands-on involvement. This lucky number involves your mental, physical, emotional, and spiritual senses. It is a powerful magnet in calendar experiences.

The total of your month, day and year of birth is the number of your destiny. It defines your path: your environment, educational opportunities, and your purpose in "the Grand Plan". You touch upon the lives of many people. Numerology's number meanings prepare you to be comfortable with the types of people and experiences that you will meet and collect.

Your destiny power number attracts what you need. Most people are not born knowing how to pinpoint congenial counterparts. The attraction is spontaneous and, once you've picked a winner, you can do it again and again. After a while, you ripen to the habit of visualizing success and letting your vibes work for you.

February 24 1957 **Alain Prost**   (19)①⑥⑧③⑥⑦

Concentrate on your *destiny number* as you mark your card - charge your positive energy - the magnetic fields defy the odds. With reinforcement, and faith, at the right moment, you'll be the long shot that wins at the wire.

YOU ARE YOUR BIRTHDAY

Instructions for LUCKY No. 3, your double number destiny vibration, follow. When you understand the numerology description of your number, you intensify its power. Numerology's single number interpretation will give you a brief outline of your special destiny.

LUCKY No. 3
HOW TO CREATE YOUR BIRTHDAY NUMBER

Calendar Month Numbers:

January = 1

February = 2

March = 3

April = 4

May = 5

June = 6

July = 7

October 10 1946   ***Chris Tarrant***   (13) (4) (4) (40) (31) (5) (?)

August = 8

September = 9

October = 10

November - 11

December = 12

Step 1.   Find your month of birth number (see values above).

Step 2.   Add your day of birth number to it.

Step 3.   Add then your year of birth number.

Step 4.   Reduce this sum to a two-digit number.

Step 5.   Play the double number.

Example: December 15, 1934

$$12 + 15 + 1934 = 1961$$

$$1 + 9 + 6 + 1 = 17$$

Play number 17 if you were born on December 15, 1934.

Example: March 22, 1946

$$3 + 22 + 1946 = 1971$$

$$1 + 9 + 7 + 1 = 18$$

Play number 18 if you were born on March 22, 1946.

November 13 1949 **Whoopi Goldberg**(41) ⑤ ② ㊼ ⑪ ⑥ ⑦

DO IT YOURSELF

Step 1.   Print your birthdate on the line below.

        _____   _____   _____

        MONTH   DAY   YEAR

Step 2.   Read the month number values above and select your month of birth number. Enter your month of birth number, your day of birth number and your year of birth number.

        _____ + _____ + _____ = _____

Step 3.   Add the numbers of your birthday that you have entered on the line above.

Step 4.

        You should have a four-digit number. Add the four numbers on the line below.

        ____ + ____ + ____ + ____ = _____

Step 5.

        LUCKY No. 3 is the double number total of Step 4.

YOUR DESTINY MEANINGS

THE NUMBER ONE - INDEPENDENCE

To develop individuality, independence and leadership through active change. Opportunities for self promotion, creativity and mental efficiency.

June 20 1952   **John Goodman**   (20) ② ③ ㊸ ⑦ ⑨ ⑦

THE NUMBER TWO - DIPLOMACY

All good things will come through patience and persistence. Wait... do not manipulate. Things... and opportunities will come to you!

THE NUMBER THREE - OPTIMISM

The lighter side of life! Giving yourself freely you will have opportunities for an expressive, creative, non-monotonous existence. Friends will further your ambitions.

THE NUMBER FOUR - APPLICATION

Opportunity to build for lasting benefit. Serving the thing at hand... you have possibilities for great attainment through teaching, serving and producing real results.

THE NUMBER FIVE - UNDERSTANDING

Frequent changes and the unexpected. Tasting, touching, smelling, feeling all the experiences that life can hold! Learning the proper use of freedom, and avoiding responsibility.

THE NUMBER SIX - ADJUSTMENT

To give valuable service to family and community... those in need. Maintaining ideals and assuming burdens and responsibilities for those who need material or spiritual help. To be protected and not to be alone through life.

November 3 1952 **Roseanne Arnold** (37)(1)(4)(31)(22)(34)(?)

THE NUMBER SEVEN - WISDOM

Opportunity to develop from within. Flourishing intuition with keen mental analysis searching for the deeper meaning of life. Awareness that to be alone is not to be lonely. To be your own best company!

THE NUMBER EIGHT - CONSTRUCTIVE POWER

To work and live among people of affluence. To use your constructive and powerful energies effectively to maintain a broad outlook... refusing all limitation!

THE NUMBER NINE - UNIVERSAL SERVICE

To serve and entertain... to be surrounded by creative, inspired and unusual people. To appeal to audiences and have concern for the masses. Expecting to feel concern for the problems of others by giving freely of yourself!

THE NUMBER ELEVEN - INSPIRATION

To bring your message to the universe! Recognition and inspiration will come to you. Without concern for the material things in life, your spirituality and intuition will always serve you.

THE NUMBER TWENTY-TWO - MATERIAL MASTER

To be involved in the universe of international commerce and politics. Improving and expanding all that comes: high power on all planes! Fame... for making contributions to the welfare of all.

January 29 1943 **Tony Blackburn**   (34) (7) (6) (47) (11) (13) (?)

CHAPTER

LUCKY No. 4

YOUR BIRTHDAY NUMBER REDUCED TO A SINGLE NUMBER

THE ESSENCE OF YOUR DESTINY

The sum and substance of your life is defined in numerology's portrayal of the elements in your birth-date. Each number paints a picture of encounters and exposures. The all-embracing total of these numbers is the essence of your destiny: your *Wisdom number.*

Reflect upon the explanation of the number of your birth month. It speaks of childhood and youth - the years between birth and the early thirties.

The day of birth number also takes a picture of your years of productivity - the years between approxi-

January 12 1932 **Des O'Connor** (29) ② ① (28) (10) (16) (?)

mately twenty-eight and fifty-six. This time span frames financial, domestic, and romantic snapshots of active interests, material growth and ripening goals. Your day of birth is a lens focusing on ambitions to be realized or discarded. It records the snapshots of the forties that are kept in the album as we put our shoulders to the wheel and push for security. The negatives are printed for the later years when we enter the untraditional, the freedom seeking, fifties. Birthdays furnish the blue ribbon photos in the gallery of life. They provide a progressive soft focus on time and age.

The birth year combines four numbers and, by each number definition, reveals the complexity of numerology's Cycle of Wisdom. It is the intensity of the addition of the four numbers, reduced to a double number, that explains the shot-in-the-arm reaction we feel before our normal, late-in-life, bodily slowdown (the single reduced number of the birth year is the essence of the Wisdom Cycle). The culmination of our expectations for golden-age security, may be foretold by understanding the single number of the year of our birth.

Each birthdate number provides nourishment for the other. The healthiest and most vibrant is the sum total. You are backing your life, when you play your birthdate number... your *wisdom number* of your life cycle.

June 18 1942 **Paul McCartney**   (14) (5) (4) (40) (22) (13) (?)

LUCKY NO. 4
HOW TO CREATE YOUR DESTINY NUMBER

Step 1   Add the two digits of LUCKY No. 3 and reduce them to a single number.

Step 2.   Play the single number.

Example: October 31, 1955 birthdate

$$10 + 31 + 1955 = 1996$$

$$1 + 9 + 9 + 6 = 25$$

25 is the double number of the birthdate.

Lucky No. 3 for 10/31/1955 is 25.

Add $2 + 5 = 7$ to find the single reduced number.

Lucky No. 4 is 7 for October 31, 1955.

Example: November 7, 1963 birthdate

$$11 + 7 + 1963 = 1981$$

$$1 + 9 + 8 + 1 = 19$$

19 is the double number of the birthdate.

Lucky No. 3 for 11/7/1963 is 19.

Add $1 + 9 = 10$ and reduce again.

Add $1 + 0 = 1$ to find the single reduced number.

Lucky No. 4 is 1 for November 7, 1963.

March 28 1944 **Diana Ross**   (20) (2) (4) (47) (11) (10) (?)

DO IT YOURSELF

Step 1.   Enter the double number of your birth-
            date on the lines below - your lucky No.
            3 number.

Step 2.   Add the digits.

            _____ + _____ = _____

Step 3.   If step 2 results in a double number,
            reduce it to a single number.

            _____ + _____ = _____

You must reduce more than one time, if necessary.

Step 4.   Play the single number of your birthdate
            for LUCKY No. 4.

IMPORTANT NOTE

If you want to use only one or two numbers, the
single reduced number of your first name letters
(Lucky No.1) and the single reduced number of your
birthdate (Lucky No. 4) are your best personal lucky
numbers.

July 12 1958 **Jennifer Saunders** (45) (9) (9) (42) (6) (35) (?)

DESTINY NUMBER MEANINGS

Destiny Number 1

Life may be a loner trip for Destiny number 1. You've got to be autonomous. Decisions that enhance your growth will be the decisions that are best for you - and you alone. You're intended to be a 'first'. The first one in your family to go to college, the first to be self-employed, the first to sail across the Atlantic in a bathtub. You are intended to break the standards that are traditional for you, and to be a progressive, courageous, ambitious, self-disciplined pioneer.

Destiny Number 2

Life will offer you opportunities for partnership in love, business and friendly relationships. To get the most out of people you will need to become the power behind the throne. Leaders need help. You are on the life path of the peacemaker (diplomat), the adaptable chairman's assistant, the accommodating friend. You must learn to follow the lead of others and put yourself under the laws of giving and receiving. You are intended to learn, to listen and to express yourself through patience and persistence.

Destiny Number 3

Life may be filled with social contacts, game-playing and opportunities to use words. To get the most out of the self-expressive people that you meet, you must be fashionable, artistic and ready to enjoy the latest fads and fancies. Workaholic, aggressive, disciplined people are not going to give you the experiences necessary for your growth. You will find your chances to shine on the stage, at a party, modelling, speaking and writing. Leave your troubles at home. Use your personality, and let friends promote you.

Destiny Number 4

Life will offer you conventional opportunities to work, build and maintain a stable lifestyle. The decisions that trigger your growth will be based on dependability, honesty and prudent management. Every year should produce tangible results from your strict attention to duty, your planning, work and doggedness. Investments in real estate, minerals and developing skilled craftsmanship will pay off. Organize yourself. Money, land investments and marriage will appreciate as you progress.

Destiny Number 5

Life will offer you opportunities to be a catalyst for change. Freedom to travel mentally and physically is necessary for your growth. Marriage and responsibilities will be burdensome. Look for people and experiences that are off the beaten track. Avoid planning for the future which will be a constantly changing scene. You are intended to meet all classes, creeds and unconventional experiences.

December 27 1948 **Gerard Depardieu** (35)(8)(1)(34)(7)(16)(?)

You will be enthusiastic, learn about them, and then become bored before you move on.

Destiny Number 6

Life will be a series of adjustments as you learn to handle responsibility and to take on the problems of family and community relationships. Your life is protected by emotional responsiveness to others and their's to you. It's a case of what goes around comes around. Others less able to cope will cross your path and you will be given opportunities to serve their practical, spiritual and emotional needs. It's up to you to maintain harmony by cheerfully providing, nurturing and producing what they need.

Destiny Number 7

Life will offer you opportunities to specialize and to learn to understand that to be alone is not to be lonely. Business, ambitions for establishment status and superficial people are not for you. Your best deals walk through the door and your power is harnessed by the opportunities that come to you. Love and serenity will be found in quiet places where your mind and spirit are free to investigate theories and develop concepts. You are intended to enjoy solitude, grow wise, prosper from meditation and knowledge.

Destiny Number 8

Life will offer you opportunities to meet ambitious

and wealthy people. Your life path is filled with opportunities to deal in commerce, professional athletics and status symbols. Big ideas and big business will make you an investor in art on the practical side; art for arts sake is not for you. The key to benefitting from the movers and shakers that you meet is positiveness. Believe that you can be the next Richard Branson or Linford Christie and you will become a millionaire or notable professional athlete: Aim high, the world is your oyster.

Destiny Number 9

Life offers you opportunities to be self-sacrificing and a hero to your family, friends or the world at large. To get the most out of the charitable, humanitarian, philosophical people you meet, set an example of kindness, expertise and generosity. You will be a romantic and give your life for the benefit of art or humanity. Marriage is difficult for the number 9 doctor or thespian; saving a life or uplifting man's cultural tastes come first. You will grow far from your birthright.

DOUBLE CHECK

Do you now have two similar personal base numbers?

If yes: wheel one of the numbers!

See Chapter VII

CHAPTER

LUCKY No. 5

BIRTHDAY
CLASSIC PYRAMID

**YOUR AGE ALTERS YOUR PERSPECTIVE;
YOUR PERSPECTIVE ALTERS
YOUR VIBRATIONS**

Would the asp, had it not bitten the breast of Cleopatra, have gone into the book of unforgettable destinies? An asp who bit an Egyptian slave would have been 'snake bites man', not 'tits 'n asp'! No fanfare. No plays written nor movies made. It is not one happening or the ingredient character that changes destiny, it is the combination of all the asp-ects.

If we lived in Cleopatra's time, a resting place filled with treasures, draped with handmaidens entombed

---

January 13 1969 **Stephen Hendry** (33) ⑥ ⑤ ㉟ ⑫ ⑭ ⑦

to serve our heavenly wishes, would be the expectation from the classic pyramid. However, not all destinies are played for all the world to share, nor are our loves and hates dramatized by Shakespeare, George Bernard Shaw or John Dryden. Compared to the race most of us run, Cleopatra was a long shot.

The secret of Cleopatra's fame was that she was a catalyst for change. Nothing in life is a sure bet except change. Cleopatra was school age when she changed the face of nations. Was she aware of, or did she care, about the mess she created? Numerology teaches that every day alters our opportunities and that we must regard our age as a means for getting a perspective on timing.

In our twenties, we collect knowledge. In our thirties, we develop social relationships. In our forties, we organize our lives to build for security. In our fifties, we want to experience all that we think we have missed. In our sixties, we want comfort and we strive to live up to our personal ideals. In our seventies, we analyze, investigate our dreams of perfection and "get religion". In our eighties, we remember the physical pleasures and strive to keep up stamina. In our nineties, we are venerable; all petty values cease to exist and we counsel others from a broad perspective. Were we to reach one hundred we would all begin again! Thus the way in which we view the information offered by the classic pyramid depends upon the attitude of the moment.

March 29 1943 **John Major** (20) (2) (3) (49) (4) (20) (?)

When I slip into negativity, I remind myself that "we are perfect for what we are today. We are perfect for what we were yesterday. We are perfect for what we will be tomorrow." Our past and future are combined in the "here and now". Do we accept life as beautiful or is it beastly? The choice is always ours.

NUMEROLOGY IS A GOOD GAME

Para-sciences can help us make choices. They dare to test the challenges of time and criticism. Numerology's classic birthday pyramid has offered information since before the time of the coming of Jesus Christ it will probably be tested by Martians. It's fair game for "doubting Thomases" but does, and will continue, to be a fun game.

Play the classic pyramid technique, like a sport, with good will, and the goddess of numerology will give prominence to your vibrations.

YOU'VE GOT A COPEMATE

The pyramid is a ready reckoner. It forecasts incoming opportunities and helps you to learn from the past. Think about the number meanings and relate a perspective on your age to the experience descriptions.

August 19 1946 **Bill Clinton** (34) (7) (3) (38) (11) (48) (?)

Use the number information for self-understanding. Use the present *time span* number as your LUCKY No. 5.

The ancient pyramids are one of the seven wonders of the world. The classic destiny pyramid is the wonder of numerology. Its number forecasts are unfathomably correct. The age time spans have shown themselves accurate. The system is complex but well worth the work involved. The ancient vibrations of the pyramids have power for today's lottery too!

CLASSIC PYRAMID SYSTEM

Egyptian pyramids are flat and square at the bottom and have four triangular sides that come to a point at the top. The numerology classic pyramid will have the shape of one of the sides and rise from the flat base of your birth month, days and year numbers to meet at the point of your last cycle of life experiences. The Egyptians used pyramids as royal tombs to enhance a life after death. Numerologists use the classic pyramid as a tree of life that points to pinnacles of experience within your destiny.

October 13 1925 **Margaret Thatcher** (38) (2) (4) (40) (13) (27) (?)

INSTRUCTIONS

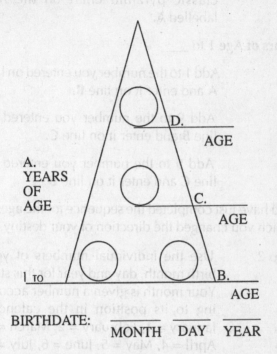

A.
YEARS
OF
AGE

C.
AGE

D.
AGE

1 TO

B.
AGE

BIRTHDATE: ——— ——— ———
MONTH   DAY   YEAR

Step 1.   Use the single number total of your
           birthdate (LUCKY No. 4) for this
           calculation.
           Subtract this single number from 36.
           The resulting number represents the age
           at which you ended the first pinnacle in
           life - your Youth Cycle.

February 6 1911 **Ronald Reagan** (28)(1)(1)(20)(2)(14)(?)

A.   Enter the resulting number in the blank
                classic pyramid chart on the line
                labelled **A**.

Years of Age 1 to _____

B.   Add 1 to the number you entered on line
                A and enter it on line **B**.

C.   Add 9 to the number you entered on
                line **B** and enter it on line **C**.

D.   Add 9 to the number you entered on
                line **C** and enter it on line **D**.

You have just completed the sequence for the ages at
which you changed the direction of your destiny.

Step 2.   Use the individual numbers of your
                birth month, day and year for this step.
                Your month is given a number accord-
                ing to its position in the calendar.
                January = 1, February = 2, March = 3,
                April = 4, May = 5, June = 6, July = 7,
                August = 8, September = 9, October =
                10, November = 11, December = 12.

                Your day of birth number is used as is.
                Do NOT reduce a double number to a
                single number.

                Reduce your year of birth to a double
                number by adding the four digits.

November 21 1945 **Goldie Hawn** (34)(7)(4)(33)(6)(30)(?)

Example: 1945: 1 + 9 + 4 + 5 = 19

1928: 1 + 9 + 2 + 8 = 20

1967: 1 + 9 + 6 + 7 = 23

Print the numbers of your month, day and year of birth on the indicated lines, at the base of the pyramid.

Here's the tricky part. Examples follow the instructions. PANIC NOT!

Step 3.

A.   Add your month of birth number to your day of birth number and enter the sum in the circle closest to line **A**.

B.   Add your day of birth number to your year of birth number (the double digit one you've just entered at the pyramid base) and enter the sum in the circle closest to line **B**.

C.   Add the two numbers that you entered in the **A** and **B** circles. Print the sum of the two numbers in the circle closest to line **C**.

D.   Add your month of birth number to your year of birth double-digit number and enter the sum in the circle closest to line **D**.

March 17 1951 **Kurt Russell** (16)⑦④㊱⑨⑧❓

Step 4.   You know your own age. Look at your
               own classic pyramid chart. Find the
               line - **A**, **B**, **C**, or **D**, - that has the
               number closest to your age without
               going over it. For example, if your line
               B says 30 and your line **C** says 39 and
               you are now 38 years of age, use line
               B because it's closest to your age with-
               out going over it. Note the number in
               the circle next to this line. Any age
               before the age printed on line **A** or after
               the age on line **D** selects the number
               in the circle closest to its age line.

               LUCKY No. 5 is the number in the circle
               closest to your age span.

CHECK AGAIN

Do you have two similar base
numbers?

If yes: wheel one of the numbers

See Chapter VII

DIANA, PRINCESS OF WALES
CLASSIC PYRAMID

Would DIANA, a woman of many facets and experiences, speculate with Psychic Whoopee? Why not? Moses, Julius Caesar and Pulitzer Prize-winning playwright David Mamet did!

July 1, 1961

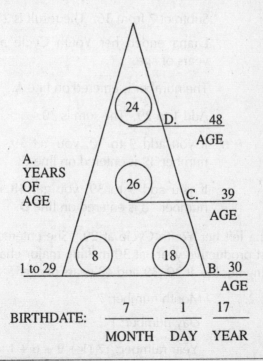

A.
YEARS
OF
AGE

24

D. __48__
AGE

26

C. __39__
AGE

8   18

1 to 29   B. __30__
AGE

BIRTHDATE: __7__   __1__   __17__
              MONTH   DAY   YEAR

Step 1.   Diana's birthdate

July 1, 1961

Month: July = 7

Day = 1 (Reduce double numbers to a single number).

Year = 1961 = 1 + 9 + 6 + 1 = 17, 1 + 7 = 8

Total: 7 + 1 + 8 = 16, 1 + 6 = 7

Subtract 7 from 36. The result is 29

Diana ended her Youth Cycle at 29 years of age.

A.   The number is entered on line **A**.

B.   Add 1 to 29. The sum is 30.

C.   If you add 9 to 30, you get 39. The number 39 is entered on line **C**.

D.   If you add 9 to 39, you get 48. The number 48 is entered on line **D**.

Diana left her Youth Cycle at 29. She entered her most productive years at 30 making major changes during her life at 30, 39 and 48 years of age.

Step 2.   Month number: 7

Day number: 1

Year number: 17 (1 + 9 + 6 + 1 = 17)

August 23 1970 **River Phoenix** (36)(9)(8)(48)(12)(31)(?)

For Diana's classic pyramid, the numbers 7, 1 and 17 are entered in the birthdate spaces at the pyramid base.

Step 3.

A.   Add Diana's month and day numbers.
            7 + 1 = 8.

            The number 8 is entered in the circle closest to line **A**.

B.   Add Diana's day and year numbers.
            1 + 17 = 18.

            The number 18 is entered in the circle closest to line **B**.

C.   Add the sum of the numbers entered in the circles for A and B for Diana.
            8 + 18 = 26.

D.   Add Diana's month number 7 to her year number 17. 7 + 17 = 24.

            The number 24 is entered in the circle closest to line **D**.

Step 4.   Diana should play the number in the circle nearest her current age. In 1995 Diana will be 34 years old. The age 30 on line B is closest to her age in 1995. In 1995 Diana should play number 18.

            LUCKY No, 5 for Diana is number 18.

October 28 1967 **Julia Roberts**   (17) (8) (5) (16) (7) (38) (?)

INTERPRETATIONS FOR THE CIRCLED NUMBERS IN THE CLASSIC PYRAMID

The circled numbers describe the types of people and experiences that you will meet during the ages closest to them.

Numbers 1, 10, 19, 28, 37, 46, 55, 64, 73, 82, 91.

Whatever your age, you will have the opportunity to develop independence. The people you meet will spark your individuality, creativity and inventiveness. In business expect to meet people who don't like taking orders, who make changes that improve their progress. You will learn how to go it alone or be given positions of leadership.

In sex, love, marriage, domestic and family relationships, expect to meet people who assert themselves. Happiness and financial stability depend upon the strength of your ego, your personal ambition, and whether you are able to "have the courage of your convictions."

Numbers 2, 11, 20, 29, 38, 47, 56, 65, 74, 83, 92.

Whatever your age, you will have the opportunity to develop your sensitivity. The people you meet will spark your humility, adaptability and kindness. In business expect to meet supportive partners, people who assist leaders and prefer a peaceful environment. You will learn to be patient.

August 29 1958 **Michael Jackson** (33)(6)(9)(15)(6)(7)(?)

In sex, love, marriage, domestic and family relation-ships, expect to meet detail-minded, helpful and non-aggressive people. Happiness and financial stability depend upon your ability to be diplomatic, to main-tain friendly alliances and to fit in with groups.

Numbers 3, 12, 21, 30, 39, 48, 57, 66, 75, 84, 93.

Whatever your age, you will have the opportunity to develop self expression. The people you meet will spark your personality, artistic talents and ability to be optimistic. In business expect to meet communi-cators: people who like attention, variety and imaginative projects. You will learn to use words to your advantage.

In sex, love, marriage, domestic and family relation-ships, expect to meet people who are charming, fashionable and who love beauty. Happiness and financial stability depend upon whether you are up-to-date, attractive and seek out social contacts. The mail and telephone are your tools for success.

Numbers 4, 13, 22, 31, 40, 49, 58, 67, 76, 85, 94.

Whatever your age, you will have the opportunity to develop practicality. The people you meet will spark your common sense, patience and material values. You will learn the importance of saving money, to collect tangible assets and to work for everything that you get. In business expect to meet managerial, orderly, emotionally self-limiting people.

February 27 1932 **Elizabeth Taylor**   (43)(7)(4)(44)(8)(17)(?)

In sex, love, marriage, domestic and family relationships, expect to meet people who are proper, traditional and constructive. Happiness and financial stability depend upon whether you are able to love your work.

Numbers 5, 14, 23, 32, 41, 50, 59, 68, 77, 86, 95.

Whatever your age, you will have the opportunity to develop adaptability. The people you meet will spark your sensuality, impulsiveness and desire for the freedom to be adventurous. You will learn to let go of people and things that no longer sustain your enthusiasm. In business expect to meet entrepreneurs, and encounter unconventional work environments.

In sex, love, marriage, domestic and family relationships, expect to meet with expansive ideas, uncertainty, a focus upon physical pleasures. Happiness and financial stability depend upon whether you are irresponsible, exposed to too many unexpected changes or get caught up in "sex and the senses."

Numbers 6, 15, 24, 33, 42, 51, 60, 69, 78, 87, 96.

Whatever your age, you will have the opportunity to develop a sense of responsibility. The people you meet will spark your desire to have "roots," harmony at home and business, and to serve in order to make people and environments more comfortable. You will learn to assume positions of trust and to adhere to your personal ideals. In business expect to meet situations and people that demand that you adjust yourself for the good of the group, that expect service and give you their burdens.

In sex, love, marriage, domestic and family relationships, expect to meet parental types of people who offer protection but expect that you will take care of them too. Happiness and financial stability depend upon developing a "live and let live" attitude and upon living harmoniously with other people.

Numbers 7, 16, 25, 34, 43, 52, 61, 70, 79, 88, 97.

Whatever your age, you will have the opportunity to develop an investigative, analytical approach to yourself. The people you meet will spark your intellect, quality and consciousness and need to do things perfectly. You will learn to be aware of personal philosophies, the joy of privacy, and how to be alone and be your own best friend. In business expect to meet legalistic, questioning and authoritative specialists.

In sex, love, marriage, domestic and family relationships, expect to be a loner who is able to find soul mates. Happiness and financial stability depend upon your ability to know when to be silent, how to specialize or concentrate on one career or business, and to realize that it is in your best interest to be non-materialistic.

Numbers 8, 17, 26, 35, 44, 53, 62, 71, 80, 89, 98.

Whatever your age, you will have the opportunity to

develop executive judgment, efficiency and material ambitions. The people you meet will spark your involvement with commercial activity. You will learn to assume control, to work to be influential and affluent. In business expect to meet company presidents, self-made leaders and achievers in all professions and industries.

In sex, love, marriage, domestic and family relationships, expect to meet people who are impatient with trifles, inefficiency and humbleness. Happiness and financial stability depend upon your stamina, courage and determination to aim high.

Numbers 9, 18, 27, 36, 45, 54, 63, 72, 81, 90.

Whatever your age you will have the opportunity to develop a broad-scoped philosophy. The people you meet will spark your ability to be empathetic, generous and noble. You will learn to serve others with humanitarian or impersonal love that requires selflessness. In business expect to meet notables: inspired communicators; people who demand quality and skill of performance.

In sex, love, marriage, domestic and family relationships, expect to meet good lovers, and people who are gifted with wisdom. Happiness and financial stability depend upon having the freedom to give service outside of personalized relationships, and to enjoy the cultural growth that is offered. This number travels far from its birthright in the Youth Cycle.

May 23 1933 **Joan Collins**   (13) (4) (9) (44) (8) (21) (?)

CHAPTER

LUCKY No. 6

THE CALENDAR DAY NUMBER

Each day has a single number vibration that describes the types of actions people will take, the directions of industry and the focus of governments. The high energy affects all of us. So when you play a lottery of multiple numbers, it is essential that you tie your numbers into the calendar day number. Here's how you do it.

Step 1.   Select the calendar month number: January = 1, February = 2, March = 3, April = 4, May = 5, June = 6, July = 7, August = 8, September = 9, October = 10, November = 11, December = 12.

Step 2.   Add the calendar day number.

Step 3.   Plus the total of the calendar year numbers.

March 19 1955 **Bruce Willis** (22)(4)(1)(42)(6)(39)(?)

Step 4.   You may reduce this to a single number
            or wheel it (See Chapter VII).

Example: November 19, 1994

            Month number: 11

            Day number: 19

            Year number: 23 (1 + 9 + 9 + 4 = 23)

            11 + 19 + 23 = 53, 5 + 3 = 8

Alternatives: 17, 26, 35 and 44

November 19, 1994 is a number 8 calendar day, a
day to include number 8 on your entry.

The back-up numbers are 17, 26, 35 or 44 i.e. any
double number that when added together reduces to
a number 8. Example: 35: 3 + 5 = 8.

If you cannot play with the number 8 – for example,
because 8 is one of your personal numbers, and you
cannot repeat it you should play the alternatives,
especially if you buy more than one lottery ticket.

Example: January 5, 1999

            Month number: 1

            Day number: 5

            Year number: 28 (1 + 9 + 9 + 9 = 28)

            1 + 5 + 28 = 34 = 7

Alternatives: 16, 25, 34 and 43

January 5, 1999, is a number 7 calendar day, a day
to include number 7 on your card.

January 30 1951 **Phil Collins**   (43) (7) (3) (47) (11) (46) (?)

The back-up numbers 16, 25, 34 and 43 may be considered as an alternate if you cannot play number 7 because you are already using it as a personal number especially if you buy more than one lottery ticket.

Example: August 8, 2001

Month number: 8

Day number: 8

Year number: 3 (2 + 0 + 0 + 1 = 3)

$8 + 8 + 3 = 19$, $1 + 9 = 10$,

$1 + 0 = 1$

Alternatives: 10, 19, 28, 37 and 46

August 8, 2001 = a number 1 calendar day, a day to include number 1 on your card.

The back-up numbers 10, 19, 28, 37 and 46 may be considered as an alternate number if you cannot play number 1 because it has already been selected as one of your personal numbers. If you purchase more than one lottery ticket, use the alternate with your personal numbers.

For easy reference:

1994 = 23	1998 = 27
1995 = 24	1999 = 28
1996 = 25	2000 = 2
1997 = 26	2001 = 3

MEANINGS FOR CALENDAR NUMBERS

Here are the number meanings for the calendar days and years. You may want to use the day numbers for other pastimes, and you will find cooperation from your associates and family when you gear yourself to using the vibes that are offered for a given day.

NUMBER 1.

Expect to meet and read about people and experiences that are inventive, exploratory and creative. The focus is upon new concepts in business and government. It is a time for "firsts."

We can relate to the influence of calandar years too. Think about the year 1945 ($1 + 9 + 4 + 5 = 19: 1 + 9 = 10: 1 + 0 = 1$), a number 1 calendar year, marking the end of the Second World War and the election of a Labour government heralding the Welfare State. 1945 was also the year of the division of India, creating the democracies of India and Pakistan signalling the end of the British Empire.

So what other "firsts" were there in Number 1 years?

In 55 BC Julius Caesar arrived in Britain bringing the country within the Roman Empire. In 1486, Dias rounded the Cape of Good Hope opening up the East. In 1549 the first English Prayer Book was published. The first race meeting at Royal Ascot was in 1711.

The Labour Party was founded in 1900. In 1909,

Louis Bleriot made the first flight across the Channel in an aeroplane he designed himself. In 1945, again, the first biros (ballpoint pens) were being marketed as the first atom bombs were being dropped on Japan. In 1963, Gordon Cooper, the astronaut, first piloted a spacecraft back to earth.

As for "creativeness", in 1495 Leonardo Da Vinci completed "The Last Supper" and in 1972 Burt Reynolds posed for the first mass-market nude male centrefold in Cosmopolitan magazine.

NUMBER 2.

Expect people to be more receptive and co-operative ventures to be highlighted. Governments are involved with treaties, pacts and negotiations. The focus is on maintenance, statistics and gathering information.

In 1469 Machiavelli was born. The Spanish Inquisition convened in 1478. Saroujah Dowlah negotiated with the East India Company by incarcerating his opponents in the Black Hole of Calcutta in 1756.

In 1649, the Parliament under Oliver Cromwell, deposed Charles 1, and beheaded him.

More recently, in 1937, Hitler repudiated the war guilt clause of the Treaty of Versailles which was negotiated, wait for it, in 1919 (another number 2 year)! In 1946, the United Nations General Assembly met for the first time. The Warsaw Pact followed in

March 29 1964 *Elle Macpherson* (16) (7) (1) (52) (7) (49) (?)

1955. In 1991 the Berlin Wall came down and Eastern Europe threw off the yoke of communism. So number 2 years have political consequences. Slavery was, finally, abolished in 1865.

VAT was introduced in 1973, a number 2 year, the year for statistics and bureaucracy.

NUMBER 3.

Expect fashion, entertainment and adult games to be in focus. The world rotates to the heartbeat of a child and people prefer to be naive. Money, energy and pleasures are scattered. People are restless and un-concentrated. The universe wants to play at random and have a cataclysmic good time.

In 1470 the printing press, heralding mass-publishing, was introduced in Paris. In 1596, Descartes,("I think, therefore I am"), was born. In 1605 Guy Fawkes tried to blow up Parliament, and thereby, created Bonfire Night which has been celebrated on the 5th November ever since. Fireworks also feature in the 1812 Symphony to glorify Napoleon's defeat at the gates of Moscow... adult games!

Money: 1929 was the year of the Wall Street stock-market crash; enough said.

Entertainment: Denis Compton scored 18 centuries in 1947. Elvis Presley "arrived" in 1956 with Heart-break Hotel. The Beatles were at their zenith in 1965. Madonna was the 'queen' in 1992... definitely a vintage year, and what about the 1947 wine vintage in France; a "Great Year".

NUMBER 4.

People and experiences come down to earth and must be stabilized after the fun and games of Number 3 years. Work is the answer. Rules and regulations are instituted to ensure a more solid future. Wars are fought to give countries firmer constitutions.

1066, the Battle of Hastings: William the Conquerer, the Norman Conquest. Need more be said? The defeat of the Spanish Armada in 1588. Need more be said?

1615, Gallileo was tried when he claimed that the earth moved around the sun, a law of nature that the Pope denied.

As for work, Tower Bridge was opened in 1894.

To square the circle of Number 4 years, the Russians, with Sputnik 1, put a space dog into orbit around the earth. The Space Age had begun. Gallileo (1615), "but it does move", was right!

NUMBER 5.

Expansions unconventional happenings and sensational headlines greet this number year which is intended to rejuvenate the public. Chances are taken - speculations flourish. New psychologies, metaphysical interests and political advertising campaigns bring on new trends. It is a "trendy" and variety filled year. Number 5 years bring about transitions by overthrowing traditions or sparking assassinations and warmongering to churn up public interest.

In 1508 Martin Luther nailed his "theses" to the cathederal door at Wurtemburg. Sensational headlines at the time which sparked the Reformation.

Anti-French propaganda was generated after Nelson's victory at Trafalgar in 1805. His monument is a testimony to that chauvinism. In 1940, the Battle of Britain provided the same rallying cry in "the darkest hour". Similarly, the Six Day War in 1967 was, not only a brilliant campaign but the epitome of public relations for the Israelis... as was the freeing of the hostages at Entebbe airport in 1976.

What of 1976? 4000 killed in an earthquake in Turkey, and an accidently exploded atmospheric Chinese nuclear device spread radiation throughout the Northern Hemisphere. Was it not in 1913 that Archduke Ferdinand was assassinated in Sarajevo, the trigger for the start of The Great World War of 1914-18.

Number 5 years are never dull!

NUMBER 6.

Marriage, domestic problems and internal affairs are the focus in world countries. Finances are problematic. Children's and pensioner welfare projects that

April 9 1957 **Seve Ballesteros**   (15) (6) (6) (35) (8) (31) (?)

provide comforts and improved conditions are instituted and augmented. Home products sales flourish, groups and clubs attract joiners, and stories about local politics hit the papers.

In 1815 the Battle of Waterloo was fought, having been won, according to the Iron Duke on the playing fields of Eton. Napoleon left for domestic solitude in St. Helena. In 1869 the Suez Canal was opened improving trade with India only to find itself totally closed again in 1959 after the Suez crisis the previous year with vast international financial consequences.

In 1950 there was good news after the exigencies of the War. It was the end of soap rationing and, even better news, the end of sweet rationing as the country celebrated with the Festival of Britain.

1788 was perhaps the biggest typical event of this Number 6 year with the departure of the First Fleet for Botany Bay to colonize Australia with inmates of London's gaols. A welfare project!

NUMBER 7.

Existing conditions get a fine going-over and things that are hidden beneath the surface and have underlying meanings attract attention. Things that are already set in motion are perfected. International finances depend upon the stability of the preceding year, and will be on the upswing during the year if the economy is problematic. All earth products do well, innovative electronic products are introduced. Discoveries are in focus. People take an analytic stance. Newspapers are loaded with stories about law trials and agricultural productivity.

1789, the fall of the Bastille, the French Revolution and Mme.Defarge doing her knitting at the steps of the guillotine was a Number 7 year. The masses decided to improve their lot and overthrow the Ancien Regime of the feudal King and the aristocracy. "They got a going over".

1492, Columbus discovered America. Magellan, who was first to sail around Cape Horn, died. 1564, Shakespeare was born. All were auspicious within a Number 7 year, while the San Francisco earthquake was an example of trauma in 1906. Amundsen's fix on the North Pole was a discovery of electro-magnetism in the same year.

When could Tulip Mania, when tulips became currency, have occured other than in a Number 7 year? The year was 1636 and it even caused hyper inflation... things perfected.

Number 7 years introduce the reasons we take action in the future year.

NUMBER 8.

Businesses expand, money is king and warlike fights for survival take place. People are involved in wheeling and dealing for major financial results. Stock markets increase activity. Wall Street and Footsie 100 records are broken. International trade expands through breakthroughs in engineering, conglomerate operations and government power plays. Legislators are busy keeping up with prosperity or depression. Sports and athletics make headlines. Physical fitness is fashionable and people want to keep up their stamina to support their ambitions. Everyone wants control and their seems to be more Chiefs than Indians.

"T'was ever thus". As with the 1980's so with the 1880's and the 1780's.. They were decades of boom followed by bust. In the 1780's Warren Hastings and the East India Company were making so much money in India that England chose to hold India while it allowed the 13 Colonies across the Atlantic to go their own way... not a good long term decision! In the 1880's, with the Industrial Revolution in full swing the British Empire reached its apogee. Anthony Trollope wrote of the 1880's as a time of greed and self-interest in "The Way We Live Now".

In 1871, the year of the Franco-Prussian War Bismark's armies reached the gates of Paris and the Paris Commune overthrew the government to create the Third Republic. 1952, Queen Elizabeth acceded to the throne. 1907, at the Second Peace Conference of the Hague, 46 countries adopted the 10 conventions of war.

March 12 1946 **Liza Minelli**   ㉑③①㉟⑧㉓⑦

Atmospheric hydrogen bomb experiments took place in the Pacific in 1952. In 1961, the biggest ever 50-megaton explosion by the Russians took place, the year of President Kennedy's ill-fated invasion of the Bay of Pigs. In 1970, Biafra lost its fight for independence from Nigeria while Rhodesia made it's Unilateral Declaration of Independence from Britain.

But the 80's were the epitome of Number 8 years... business greed, excess and self interest. Lots of activity......and years of the Yuppy. Politically think of William Pitt (1880's), Bismark(1880's) or the Thatcher, Reagan economics of the 1980's .

NUMBER 9.

"Brotherly love" are the watch words. People and their governments want an end to war, international hatreds and vendettas. Nations work to end unsatisfactory relationships and people are supportive in negotiations to clean out dead issues and clear the decks for peace. Humanitarian projects, the medical profession and business inventories aid in the elimination of intolerance and greed. The communications industries - TV, fashion, publishing, radio, theatre, postal and telecommunications, as well as noble and notable personalities, attract attention.

King John and the Barons signed Magna Carta in 1215 at Runnymeade... the first parliament (about tax and how much the King could levy... what else!) to be forced upon the King: and the first symbolic Bill of Rights.

In 1170, after Thomas A'Beckett was murdered in Canterbury cathedral, King Henry II crawled the length of the aisle being flogged by the monks in penance and contrition. In 1413, St. Joan of Arc was burned at the stake to become a martyr and symbol of nationalism for the French.

In 1620 the pilgrims left on the Mayflower for the New World to achieve freedom of worship. In 1521 Henry VIII was made Defender of the Faith, ironically by the Pope who was to excommunicate him!

In 1917, there was the Russian Revolution, when the Bolsheviks finally overthrew the Tsarist tyranny. The Americans entered the 1st World War with the French and the British.

Freud's 'Introduction to Psychoanalysis' was published and became the psychiatrists bible, and a gift to psychotherapy... a book that changed perceptions.

In 1935 there was Roosevelt's "New Deal" calling for social security, improved housing and equitable taxation. In 1944, the United Nations was proposed and both the International Monetary Fund and the World Bank were created.

Stalin died in 1953, the Queen was crowned and England won the Ashes! The Korean war ended. In 1971 China was invited to join the United Nations.

February 2 1940 **David Jason** (22)(4)(9)(19)(27)(16)(?)

In 1980, the Shah died, having been deposed the previous year. In 1980, Mao's rule with the "Gang of Four" ended and at Camp David the Israelis and the Egyptians signed the Accord brokered by President Carter. It was a year of reconciliation and peace.

Again in 1980, the "right to life" abortion issue became a major controversy and the causes of feminism became politically correct.

The 1990's need to be a decade of rethinking, caring and reconciliation. It's no accident that the current political issues worldwide are solving the Bosnian crisis, feeding refugees in Africa, helping the poor and the aged to healthcare, reducing unemployment and improving educational opportunities for "the young". The 9s should help but it is a sobering thought that the only calendar Number 9 year in this decade is 1999... the year of the Millenium.

The whole world vibrates to numerical universal law and people are affected by the trends described by the numbers of the calendar year. Each calendar month within the year brings a change to the international focus, and each day in the month has an influence all its own.

CHAPTER

WHEELING THE NUMBERS

The phrase "wheeling the numbers" applies to the lottery and to games that offer the option to play more than one number. The numerology system for wheeling the numbers allows you to play your personal essence number vibrations in double or triple number versions; four digit numbers are possible too. You are able to select a number that corresponds to your personal single number. You may also choose a double or triple number from your personal number wheel and tie it in with the calendar day number to create your personal wheel of good fortune.

It's necessary to have alternate numbers to play. Your name number, ABRACADABRA numbers and birth-date numbers may include duplicates. Don't lose your concentrated energy by picking a number at random. Pick the same vibration in double or triple

October 7 1939 **Clive James**   (24) (6) (9) (39) (12) (32) (?)

number form from the single number wheel. Wheeling your personal first name and birthdate numbers brings in winners when the calendar day timing is right.

IT'S TOO DIFFICULT TO BE YOUR OWN SHRINK OR CREATE A SYSTEM

Why do therapists go to other therapists? Because they cannot see the "wood for the trees" when their own problems arise. When you do not know which numbers to play, don't become inventive. It is unlikely that you will intuitively find a technique that brings up your number vibrations consistently. You will probably get caught up in your own creativity, and your intuition will not serve you well. "Physician, heal thyself" sounds fine for a professional, but it doesn't work for shrinks, and attempting to be a shrink is unlikely to work for you.

THE LOGICAL SYSTEM FOR SELECTING ALTERNATE NUMBERS

The chance that duplicates will arise in numerology personal numbers is iffy, but possible. You cannot play a number twice on the same lottery ticket. Please do NOT devise your own system. Numerology is the only system based upon universal number

March 26 1931 **Leonard Nimoy** (33)(6)(8)(43)(7)(17)(?)

vibrations. It is the only system that includes your personal numbers and combines with calendar numbers. Common sense and beating the odds do not go hand in hand, but there is logic in using a tool that has its foundation in the gaming vibration.

You may be tempted to multiply one of your numbers by itself or use two of the same number as a double number. Wrong!

For example: number 4. Multiplying 4 by itself turns it into a 7 (4 x 4 = 16; 16: 1 + 6 = 7). That's a no-no. If you turn 4 into 44, that's an 8(4 + 4 = 8).Number 8 is not as bad a bet as 7 if you have a 4 in your personal numbers. But you lose the essence of the 4 and decrease the intensity of your personal electricity.

Any system that changes the value of your number alters its music. When you play a different number, it corresponds to playing a note on a piano that doesn't blend with the accompanying chord. You hit a flat! You're not singing your own song. You're humming a note that complements another person's musical progressions. That person ends up with a resounding orchestration of the melody, a richer sound. In practical terms, that person gets the energy benefit of your choice.

If you need an alternate number, choose it from the numbers wheel listing for your personal number. The lower the number, the closer it is to its essence. For example, you will notice that the wheeled numbers for the number 5 are 14, 23, 32, 41, 50, etc. You may play any of these numbers, and the 14 is the closest to the essence of 5. (The wheeled numbers are those whose digits add up to the single number in question).

TIPSTER'S TIP

As you glance through the Numbers Wheel for your personal name or birthdate single number, you may realize that the calendar day number is included in the two or three digits. Play that number. For example, if one of your personal numbers is 9, you have 18, 27, 36, 45, etc., to chose from as a wheeled number. But if the lottery is being drawn on a 7 calendar day, you probably want to choose 27 (it has a 7 in it) for your bet.

THE QUINTESSENCE OF YOU -
A TRIPLE NUMBER CHOICE

Your QUINTESSENCE number is your first name and birthdate numbers combined. The QUINTESSENCE number is a good choice when only one triple number is required to play a game and when you only make one play.

Step 1.   Here's how to find your QUINTES-
                SENCE number. Combine the single
                numbers of your first name and birth-

date. Example: If your first name number is 5 and your birthdate number is 3, add them together - the sum is 8 (5 + 3 = 8).

Your LUCKY No. 1 and your LUCKY No. 4 as described in the preceding chapters, when combined, are called your QUINTESSENCE number.

Your QUINTESSENCE number must always be a single number. If for example, your name and birthday numbers are 7 and 8 (which add up to 15), you must reduce this to a single number (1 + 5 = 6).

Step 2.

Look through the Numbers Wheel for your single QUINTESSENCE number to select the three-digit number that includes them both. Sounds complicated, but it isn't.

Example: First name = 5 and birthdate = 3. Three-digit numbers from the Numbers Wheel for 8 are 134, 251 and 701. These are NOT your best choices. Play a triple number that includes your two personal numbers - 953, 395, 350 or 530, for example.

If there is more than one three-digit number that includes the two personal numbers, use the lower. Example: 530 is higher that 350. Both are included in the number 8 wheel. You play number 350 because it is lower, and closer to the original single essence number, UNLESS there is some reason you cannot play that number. If that is so, use the next lower number.

PLEASE NOTE: The three-digit wheeled version of your QUINTESSENCE number is used only when making one triple number play. You may use your single-digit QUINTESSENCE number for playing when single numbers are required.

Single numbers that result from numerology's first name and birthdate systems, and their wheeled back-ups, may be used to place ANY type of bet.

IN A NUTSHELL...

Wheeled numbers 1 through 9 are listed below. You may choose to play your highest vibrations: the first name number and the birthdate number in combinations of two and three digit numbers as alternate choices.

Instructions for finding your first name number are included in Chapter I (LUCKY No. 1) and for your birthdate number in Chapter III (LUCKY No. 3).

April 27 1944 **Michael Fish** (33) (6) (9) (49) (13) (4) (?)

NOTE: If your home address, vehicle licence plate, telephone, office extension - or any of the constant numbers in your daily life - is the same as a wheeled number of your name or birthdate number, you are attracting your fortunate, supportive vibrations. When there is a toss-up: if you want to make a decision about which house to buy or which store to rent, for example, select the one that includes your personal numbers or that adds up to the sum of your personal number and birthdate numbers. You will be attracting the people and experiences that have your vibrations.

NOTE: The calendar day number for the lottery drawing may be wheeled too. That number is your lottery LUCKY No. 6. The day that you play determines the calendar timing vibration.

If you are able to buy your ticket on a calendar date with a single number that is the same as your QUINTESSENCE number, do it. If you can select a calendar date to purchase that has the same number as your QUINTESSENCE number, it adds intensity to your vibrations. Remember! Do NOT play a calendar date number for the day you buy your lottery ticket. LUCKY No. 6, the calendar timing choice for the lottery, is based upon *the date that the lottery numbers are drawn*.

Now you have an adaptable system for most gambling games that require different types of play. It's time to spin the wheels of good fortune!

August 16 1967 **Ulrika Jonsson** (27) (9) (2) (47) (11) (24) (?)

NUMBERS WHEEL

NOS.	1	2	3	4	5	6	7	8	9
	10	11	12	13	14	15	16	17	18
	19	20	21	22	23	24	25	26	27
	28	29	30	31	32	33	34	35	36
	37	38	39	40	41	42	43	44	45
	46	47	48	49	50	51	52	53	54
	55	56	57	58	59	60	61	62	63
	64	65	66	67	68	69	70	71	72
	73	74	75	76	77	78	79	80	81
	82	83	84	85	86	87	88	89	90
	91	92	93	94	95	96	97	98	99
	100	101	102	103	104	105	106	107	108
	109	110	111	112	113	114	115	116	117
	118	119	120	121	122	123	124	125	126
	127	128	129	130	131	132	133	134	135
	136	137	138	139	140	141	142	143	144
	145	146	147	148	149	150	151	152	153
	154	155	156	157	158	159	160	161	162
	163	164	165	166	167	168	169	170	171
	172	173	174	175	176	177	178	179	180
	181	182	183	184	185	186	187	188	189
	190	191	192	193	194	195	196	197	198
	199	200	201	202	203	204	205	206	207
	208	209	210	211	212	213	214	215	216
	217	218	219	220	221	222	223	224	225
	226	227	228	229	230	231	232	233	234
	235	236	237	238	239	240	241	242	243
	244	245	246	247	248	249	250	251	252
	253	254	255	256	257	258	259	260	261
	262	263	264	265	266	267	268	269	270
	271	272	273	274	275	276	277	278	279
	280	281	282	283	284	284	286	287	288
	289	290	291	292	293	294	295	296	297
	298	299	300	301	302	303	304	305	306
	307	308	309	310	311	312	313	314	315
	316	317	318	319	320	321	322	323	324
	325	326	327	328	329	330	331	332	333
	334	335	336	337	338	339	340	341	342

September 5 1946 **Freddie Mercury** (42)(6)(1)(34)(7)(29)(?)

NOS.	1	2	3	4	5	6	7	8	9
	343	344	345	346	347	348	349	350	351
	352	353	354	355	356	357	358	359	360
	361	362	363	364	365	366	367	368	369
	370	371	372	373	374	375	376	377	378
	379	380	381	382	383	384	385	386	387
	388	389	390	391	392	393	394	395	396
	397	398	399	400	401	402	403	404	405
	406	407	408	409	410	411	412	413	414
	415	416	417	418	419	420	421	422	423
	424	425	426	427	428	429	430	431	432
	433	434	435	436	437	438	439	440	441
	442	443	444	445	446	447	448	449	450
	451	452	453	454	455	456	457	458	459
	460	461	462	463	464	465	466	467	467
	469	470	471	472	473	474	475	476	477
	478	479	480	481	482	483	484	485	486
	487	488	489	490	491	492	493	494	495
	496	497	498	499	500	501	502	503	504
	505	506	507	508	509	510	511	512	513
	514	515	516	517	518	519	520	521	522
	523	524	525	526	527	528	529	530	531
	532	533	534	535	536	537	538	539	540
	541	542	543	544	545	546	547	548	549
	550	551	552	553	554	555	556	557	558
	559	560	561	562	563	564	565	566	567
	568	569	570	671	572	573	574	575	576
	577	578	579	580	581	582	583	584	585
	586	587	588	589	590	591	592	593	594
	595	596	597	598	599	600	601	602	603
	604	605	606	607	608	609	610	611	612
	613	614	615	616	617	618	619	620	621
	622	623	624	625	626	627	628	629	630
	631	632	633	634	635	636	637	637	639
	640	641	642	643	643	645	646	647	648
	649	650	651	652	653	654	655	656	657
	658	659	660	661	662	663	664	665	666
	667	668	669	670	671	672	673	674	675

May 20 1946 **Cher**   (25) (7) (6) (45) (9) (25) (?)

NOS.	1	2	3	4	5	6	7	8	9
	676	677	678	679	680	681	682	683	684
	685	686	687	688	689	690	691	692	693
	694	695	696	697	698	699	700	701	702
	703	704	705	706	707	708	709	710	711
	712	713	714	715	716	717	718	719	720
	721	722	723	724	725	726	727	728	729
	730	731	732	733	734	735	736	737	738
	739	740	741	742	743	744	745	746	747
	748	749	750	751	752	753	754	755	756
	757	758	759	760	761	762	763	764	765
	766	767	768	769	770	771	772	773	774
	775	776	777	778	779	780	781	783	783
	784	785	786	787	788	789	790	791	792
	793	794	795	796	797	798	799	800	801
	802	803	804	805	806	807	808	809	810
	811	812	813	814	815	816	817	818	819
	820	821	822	823	824	825	826	827	828
	829	830	831	832	833	834	835	836	837
	838	839	840	841	842	843	844	845	846
	847	848	849	850	851	852	853	854	855
	856	857	858	859	860	861	862	863	864
	865	866	867	868	869	870	871	872	873
	874	875	876	877	878	879	880	881	882
	883	884	885	886	887	888	889	890	891
	892	893	894	895	896	897	898	899	900
	901	902	903	904	905	906	907	908	909
	910	911	912	913	914	915	916	917	918
	919	920	921	922	923	924	925	926	927
	928	929	930	931	932	933	934	935	936
	937	938	939	940	941	942	943	944	945
	946	947	948	949	950	951	952	953	954
	955	956	957	958	959	960	961	962	963
	964	965	966	967	968	969	970	971	972
	973	974	975	976	977	978	979	980	981
	982	983	984	985	986	987	988	989	990
	991	992	993	994	995	996	997	998	999
	1000	1001	1002	1003	1004	1005	1006	1007	1008

CHAPTER

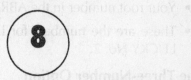

WHICH NUMBERS HAVE PRIORITY?

Your personal numbers have been discussed in the preceding chapters. If you have followed the instructions for finding your personal lucky numbers, you have six numbers to play with. You have discovered the six numbers that are luckiest for you, in most lotteries.

Your best single number choice is your QUINTESSENCE number, which is described in Chapter VII. If you only need two, three, four or five numbers to play, you need to know the order of importance of the betting numbers. It's time to sort priorities.

HOW TO PLAY LESS THAN SIX NUMBERS

The One-Number Option
- Your single-digit QUINTESSENCE number.

August 8 1953 **Nigel Mansell** (29) (2) (7) (34) (25) (26) (?)

The Two-Number Option
- Your first name single reduced number.
- Your root number in the ABRACADABRA.
- These are the numbers for LUCKY No. 1 and LUCKY No. 2.

The Three-Number Option
- Your first name single reduced number.
- Your root number in the ABRACADABRA.
- Your single number of your birthdate.
- These are the numbers for LUCKY No. 1, LUCKY No. 2 and LUCKY No. 3.

The Four-Number Option
- Your first name single reduced number.
- Your root number in the ABRACADABRA.
- Your single number of your birthdate.
- Your double number of your birthdate.
- These are the numbers for LUCKY No. 1, LUCKY No. 2, LUCKY No. 3 and LUCKY No. 4.

The Five-Number Option
- Your first name single reduced number.
- Your root number in the ABRACADABRA.
- Your single number of your birthdate.
- Your double number of your birthdate .

July 3 1962   **Tom Cruise**   (22) (4) (4) (28) (16) (10) (?)

- Your classic pyramid birthdate number.
- These are the numbers for LUCKY No. 1, LUCKY No. 2, LUCKY No. 3, LUCKY No. 4 and LUCKY No. 5.

HOW TO PLAY MORE THAN SIX NUMBERS

Play additional personal numbers and the calendar day number by wheeling the single numbers in the six-number choice.

Select the numbers for wheeling in the following order:

1. First name.
2. Single birthdate number.
3. Calendar day number that the game or lottery takes place.
4. ABRACADABRA number.

YOU'VE GOT A SYSTEM THAT JUST WON'T QUIT!

LUCKY 5 - THE PUNTER'S FRIEND

Five is the number of the swashbuckler - the risk taker - the punter. When personal numbers are unknown, 5 is always a good choice.

At a Fireman's Fair in my home town in America, many years ago, before numerology became my mainstay and my love, I spontaneously played number 5 at a booth that had a wheel of chance. The results were surprising. I played number 5 at a wheel that offered four numbers for every spin and won six out of eight with number 5 as my dollar stake. I collected thirty-eight dollars and blushed as I ran to my car.

After I became familiar with numerology's number symbols and their meanings, I understood how I intensified my connection with the wheel of chance and why number 5 kept turning up. Number 5 is the vibration of impulsiveness - the punter's natural inclination. When you are feeling free and easy - just out to have a good time - and you do not know your personal priority number, the best play is number 5.

NUMBER 8 - THE BUSINESS AND MONEY NUMBER

Number 8 is the material master of numerology. When you lease business space, check the number of the building, the floor number and the office door number. If the number is 8, or one of the numbers listed for 8 in the Numbers Wheel, you've got a chance to "reap whatever you sow".

When purchasing a house, check the address. The real estate with a number 8 essence number attracts people and experiences that are affluent and influential. You may do business from that property and/or increase the value of your investment.

Look at the calendar date when your company registration certificate was approved. If the calendar date (the sum of the month, day and year numbers), stamped by Companies House who issue business certificates, adds to a wheeled number 8, you have a business birthday that is lucky.

Any time that money and commercial ambitions are involved, the number 8 has practical, efficient, courageous energy. It adds an extra push to your ability to wheel and deal in large issues. Number 8 is not petty and attracts the power for major ambitions to come true. It requires honest toil, ethics and determination from you. However, it is the ambitious businessman's best friend and a flush of needed energy for an athlete's uniform number.

Materially competitive people share the same personality ingredients. The company director and the professional athlete have the same characteristics. The company director brings his talents to business to break last year's profit figures. The runner wants to break the tape and go home with the gold. Both professionals require self-confidence, self-discipline and enthusiasm to push themselves to their physical limits. Number 8 is the essence of great achievement and endows the bearers or users with controlling abilities and the power to succeed.

November 30 1962 **Gary Lineker** (24) (6) (8) (32) (5) (48) (?)

The numerology symbol for bringing body, mind and spirit together is number 8. In sports, where daily practice, mental concentration and an inner drive to compete to win are necessities, a number 8 on a uniform or as a starting position number adds luck to hard work. The incentive must exist in a player before number 8 can share its electricity, but 8 will come into the money or attract power when it is connected to a sports competitor.

CHECK CHECK AND CHECK AGAIN

Do you now have two similar personal lucky numbers?

If yes: wheel one of the numbers!

See Chapter VII

CHAPTER

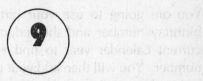

YOUR PERSONAL DAY AND PERSONAL YEAR NUMBERS

Each day your chance to board the Love Boat **'NUMEROLOGY'** changes. Personal calendar day numbers change. Your options and opportunities vary too. We all have smooth-sailing-days and days that are rough. Your personal day numbers will help you steer your adventures to safe harbours and give you more control of your life. Specifically, they will point out your lucky days for having a flutter.

Your personal numbers in numerology combine your personal birthday number and the number of the calendar year. The numbers that result are neither lucky nor unlucky. There will be good news and bad news, good things and bad things or good days and bad days. Your personal day and personal year numbers simply indicate days upon which *things happen*. They may be good, they may be bad.

October 7 1957   **Jane Torvill**   (12) ③ ⑥ ㉚ ③ ㉙ ⑦

HOW TO CREATE YOUR PERSONAL NUMBERS

You are going to use your birth month number, birthday number and the reduced number of the current calendar year to find your personal year number. You will then add your personal year number to the month and day of the calendar you are interested in knowing about. The reduced number of that addition is your personal day number.

Each year as the calendar year number changes, your personal year and day numbers change. You calculate from January 1 to December 31 of each year.

To find your personal day number you must first find your personal year number.

Personal Year: Add birth month number + birthday number + calendar year number. Add double numbers (23 = 2 + 3 = 5); reduce to a single number

Example: A June 4 birthday in 1995.

$$6 + 4 + 6 \ (1 + 9 + 9 + 5 = 24, 2 + 4 = 6)$$
$$6 + 4 + 6 = 16, 1 + 6 = 7$$

If born on June 4, your personal year number in 1995 would be a number 7.

Personal Day: Add the calendar month number + the calendar day number to your personal year number and reduce double numbers to a single number.

---

*August 3 1938 **Terry Wogan**   (34) (7) (5) (32) (14) (29) (?)*

Example: For September 17, 1995 for a person with a number 7 personal year in 1995.

> September 17 + 7 personal year
>
> 9 + 8 (1 + 7 = 8) + 7
>
> 9 + 8 + 7 = 24, 2 + 4 = 6

On September 17, 1995 with a number 7 personal year, your personal day number would be number 6.

Example: Princess Diana's personal year number in 1995 is:

Birthday: July 1

Calendar Year: 6 (1 + 9 + 9 + 5 = 24, 2 + 4 = 6)

July 1 + 6 (1 + 9 + 9 +5 = 24, 2 + 4 = 6)

7 + 1 + 6 = 14, 1 + 4 = 5

Princess Diana is in a **personal year** number 5 for 1995.

Example: Princess Diana's personal day number on May 5 1995 is:

Month number for May = 5

Day number = 5

Personal year number = 5

5 + 5 + 5 = 15, 1 + 5 = 6

On May 5, 1995 with a number 5 personal year, Diana's **personal day** number is 6.

DO IT YOURSELF

Find your personal year number:

Birth Month number: _____

Birth Day number: _____

Calendar year number: _____

Add them together: _____ + _____ + _____ = _____

and reduce to a single number.

Find your personal day number:

Calendar month number: _____

Calendar day number: _____

Personal Year: _____

Add them together: _____ + _____ + _____ = _____

and reduce to a single number.

PERSONAL YEAR AND PERSONAL DAY NUMBER MEANINGS

Number 1

Expect to meet people and experiences that help you investigate fresh ideas and require independent actions. You spark innovations! Begin the projects that you have been thinking about and base your actions on your own ego. You may have to make an unpopular decision - or two. Gather your ambition and assert yourself. *A good day* to play the lottery if it is not one of your unlucky numbers for the year.

Number 2.

Expect to meet people and experiences that require focus on details. Be diplomatic when people upstage your ideas. This is not an aggressive time span. Make new friends and reinforce your existing friendships. Don't be tempted to draw conclusions or take actions about anything yet. Be co-operative and expect the worst. *A bad day* to play the lottery.

Number 3.

Expect to meet people and experiences that trigger your imagination and make you feel optimistic. Socialize, be charming and attract attention by dressing fashionably. Pull out the stops on all your means of self-expression. Expect to have fun and allow others to enjoy your humour and good taste. You attract gifts, profit from travel and receive compliments during this time span. *A good day* to play the lottery if it is not one of your unlucky numbers for the year.

Number 4.

Expect to meet people and experiences that bring you down to earth. Work to maintain your daily sta-

July 13 1942 **Harrison Ford** (48) (3) (2) (36) (9) (23) (?)

bility... do the laundry, go to the cleaner and shop for basics. Don't waste a penny or a moment. Do the things that maintain your lifestyle. Exercise and eat a balanced diet to maintain your body. Do things that build for the future and don't expect immediate rewards or answers. *A bad day* to play the lottery.

Number 5.

Expect to meet people and experiences that feed your curiosity and restlessness. Plans will be altered. Take a break from routine activities and allow yourself to feel sensual and attract new interests. This is a time for experimentations. Get out of any ruts you feel you're in. Use this time to break habits and disciplines that you've outgrown. *A good day* to play the lottery if it is not one of your unlucky numbers for the year.

Number 6.

Expect to meet people and experiences that require time, sympathy and a helping hand. Assume positions of trust and responsibility willingly. Stay close to home. If married, focus on improving your relationship. If single, it may be possible to establish a long term commitment. Harmony and it's opposite dis-harmony are possible now. Aim to be on the giving side and your efforts will be rewarded. A *bad day* to play the lottery.

Number 7.

Expect to meet people and experiences that slow

down commercial activity and delay money. Keep social activities to a minimum. Delay shopping. Purchases you make will not please you. It is in your best interest to wait, analyze and "sleep on" any leases, contracts or agreements. Re-evaluate past judgements and future goals. Read, study and stop to smell the roses. Not a *good day* to play the lottery.

Number 8.

Expect to meet people who are businesslike and experiences that give you the opportunity to improve your finances and position. Solve problems. Focus on the affluent, influential movers and shakers in your environment. Dress to impress. Be efficient, practical and ambitious. Get the most out of yourself and everyone else. The *best day* to play the lottery.

Number 9.

Expect to meet people and experiences that require charity and noble intentions. This time takes you out of the kitchen and into the universe. Complete projects. Don't expect anything new to begin. Get rid of outmoded ideas, habits and material possessions. Be generous with those who are less fortunate than you are. This is a time to accept the inevitable and clear the decks to begin new directions in the near future. *Buy a lottery ticket for someone less fortunate than yourself...* if they win they may split the prize with you!

October 21 1962 **David Campese**   (22) (4) (9) (49) (13) (39) (?)

CHAPTER

YOUR PERSONAL "UNLUCKY" AND "CHALLENGE" NUMBERS

You have UNLUCKY days, stormy weather days when risks should not be taken. Your personal calendar day numbers will point to days when you may feel like a salmon swimming upstream, or feel that pirates are attempting to board your ship of fate.

The first is your permanent unlucky number. The second is your unlucky number for a particular year.

FIND YOUR UNLUCKY NUMBERS

To find the numbers least likely to bring you good luck.

Subtract your month of birth number from your day of birth number - whichever is smaller from the larger - and subtract your day of birth number from your personal year number - whichever is smaller from the larger.

December 31 1937 **Anthony Hopkins** (34) ⑦ ⑥ ㊺ ⑨ ㉜ ⦿

Example: Princess Diana is born on month July (7) day the first (1), and her personal year number for 1995 is number 5. **Numbers to use: 7, 1 and 5.** Thus Permanent Unlucky Number:

> Subtract: day from month, because day number is smaller.
> 7 - 1 = 6

and, Unlucky Number for 1995:

> Subtract: Birthday number 1 from personal year number 5.
> 5 - 1 = 4
> Princess Diana's Unlucky Numbers for 1995 are numbers 6 and 4.

For interest let's find Prince Charles' personal year and his personal day number on Princess Diana's birthday and his unlucky numbers for 1995.

Prince Charles, born on November 14 for 1995.

Number 1: Find personal year.

Birth month = 2 (1 + 1 = 2) + Birthday = 5 (1 + 4 = 5) + Calendar year = 6 (1 + 9 + 9 + 5 = 24, 2 + 4 = 6). 2 + 5 + 6 = 13, 1 + 3 = 4

Prince Charles' personal year number in 1995 is number 4.

Number 2: Find personal day number for July 1 in 1995 for Prince Charles. 7(July) + 1 + 4 = 12, 1 + 2 = **3.**

May 9 1936 **Glenda Jackson** (25)(7)(8)(33)(6)(24)(?)

Prince Charles' personal day number on Princess Diana's birthday in 1995 is number **3**.

For Prince Charles' unlucky numbers for 1995: Birth month number 2, birthday number 5 and personal year number 4.

The numbers to use: 2, 5 and 4.

Number 3: Subtract: 2 from 5 = 3 (permanent unlucky number).

Number 4: Subtract 4 from 5 = 1 (Remember to subtract the smaller number from the larger in all cases).

Prince Charles' unlucky numbers for 1995 are **3** and 1.

Note: Prince Charles' personal day and unlucky number 3 on Diana's birthday in 1995

Create your unlucky challenge numbers for any calendar year.

Birth month: _____ Birthday: _____ Personal year:

Permanent unlucky number:

Birth month: _____ - Birthday: _____ = _____

Unlucky number for the year:

Birthday _____ - Personal year _____ = _____

February 19 1960 **Prince Andrew** (29) (2) (6) (37) (10) (21) (?)

CHALLENGE NUMBER MATRIX

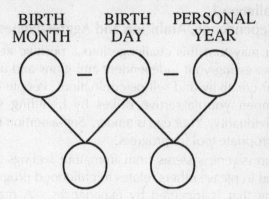

BIRTH MONTH — BIRTH DAY — PERSONAL YEAR

Unlucky number YEARS or DAYS can turn to golden years if you learn from and understand the emotionally challenging number descriptions. Your challenging number descriptions explain how to turn difficult time spans into successful and positive years and days.

When your unlucky year or day numbers come up you may wake up with one set of goals but people you meet have other fish to fry. When planning to play the lottery, quit your job or ask for a raise, consult your personal number meanings either for the go-ahead or a caution.

Steer a course each day with your personal day numbers. It's a good way to navigate!

October 15 1959 **Sarah Ferguson** (20) (2) (8) (49) (13) (39) (?)

UNLUCKY NUMBERS CHALLENGE MEANINGS

Challenge 1
Independence, Ambition and Aggressiveness

You may turn this challenge into a positive action by assessing your independent ambitions and using your creativity and self-determination. People may dampen your assertive drives by belittling your individuality. Your ego is tender. Self-assertion is an appropriate tool for progress.

Aggressiveness stems from immature feelings. The need to please others relates to childhood programming that is triggered by experiences. A mature understanding of when to be firm (not stubborn) will balance tendencies to be too forceful or too submissive, too busy or too accommodating, or too determined to win.

Challenge 2
Personalized Sensitivity and Detail Consciousness

You may turn this challenge into a positive action by tempering your emotional reactions, maintaining a broad-scope philosophy and by showing a willingness to co-operate when others assert themselves. You may be too eager to please or too self-absorbed. A less emotional, more mental approach may explain why opinions appear to be slights rather than simply observations. Pay attention to the little things. Too much self-consciousness may lead to paranoid reactions. An easy going, receptive, gentle stance balances sensitivities. Avoid being too picky or too unconcerned, too weak or too wilful, too weepy or too dry.

Challenge 3
Self-expression, Social Relationships and Imagination

You may turn this challenge into a positive action by enjoying yourself and others. Go to parties but don't be a wallflower. Attract attention with your personality, talents, and strive to be fashionable. People who talk too much or too little may annoy you.

Accepting surface values and making naive judgements bring out the negatives. The extremes are too much pizzaz or none at all. Subtlety tones down extravagance . Your sense of humour, charm and ability to play should be the focus. Aim to dress up, entertain or be entertained.

Challenge 4
Practical Reality, Conventions and Material Results

You may turn this challenge into a positive action by using common sense and discipline to work for tangible results. Too little routine or too much structure may be triggered by the people and experiences that come into your life. Conventions, traditions and practical economy are the tools for maintaining order and "doing the right thing".

This time span brings budgets, money and material objectives into focus. Take time for a break and expect to hear or see things that spark your conscience, demand a method. Ignore innovations. Concentrate or work, but avoid overdoing it to balance this challenge.

Challenge 5
Sex And The Senses, Surprises And Traditional Changes

You may turn this challenge into a positive action by adapting yourself to surprises, opening your heart and mind to the unconventional, and allowing enthusiasm. Restlessness rules the challenge. Too much or too little curiosity, fear of taking chances or a restless obsession with sex and mental fantasy are the extremes.

This is a time when accidents happen. Balance this challenge by letting go and allowing yourself to adapt to whatever comes your way. Expect the unexpected, be a non-conformist, and don't deny yourself a reasonable focus upon sex and the senses.

Challenge 6
Idealism, Sense Of Responsibility, And Emotional Ties

You may turn this challenge into a positive action by allowing others to live by their own standards and by not assuming that you are solely responsible. Family, community and business ties demand that you take on obligations and place your personal desires on hold.

You may become self-righteous, intolerant or domineering. Either extreme will challenge the harmony, peace and love in immediate relationships. A reasonable tolerance for another's weaknesses - a tease, a joke, a lighthearted hug - and a less serious, or less personalized approach brings balance.

Challenge 7
Self-deception, Faith And Realistic Appraisal

You may turn this challenge into a positive action by getting down to earth and by allowing human beings to be human. This is the time to understand mundane aspects.

Distrust, disconnection, discontent and disappointment with the real world may be self-destructive.

Listening, analyzing, asking practical questions leads to a businesslike assessment of ambitions. You must meditate upon input, respect intuition, and avoid accepting authoritative figureheads to avoid self accusations of stupidity or gullibility.

Patient reflection helps to show how you may attract what you need. Extreme reactions to this challenge may produce escapist tendencies or unnecessary changes. Be receptive and detach emotions from fact. Follow your senses. Avoid moodiness, self-depreciation, and isolation from the realities of your temporary lifestyle.

June 22 1940 *Esther Rantzen* (30)(3)(9)(42)(6)(20)(?)

Challenge 8
Money, Power, Materialism And Physical Disciplines

You may turn this challenge into a positive action by considering your reasons for accumulating money, and asking yourself whether money and/or status , has caused you to become mercenary. You may disregard the importance of organizing body, mind and spirit to achieve material ambitions.

If possessions are the only goal you are caught in an anomaly. This challenge may cause impatience with less physically or mentally self-disciplined people.

Difficulty with money, business attitudes, or physical stamina are the cautions. You may apply this challenge to commerce, material accumulation, or physical ambitions

If you strain, become intolerant with others, are selfishly ambitious, scheme for power, waste energy worrying, or find that you are motivated by emotional reactions, you are caught in the imbalance of this challenge.

Challenge 9
Humanitarian Values, Romanticism And Philosophy

You may turn this challenge into a positive action by recognizing it to be emotionally geared, requiring service and ununselfishness from you and demanding endings, never beginnings. Complete obligations, pay debts, conclude your commitments to yourself and others.

You need to be generous and give others sympathy, compassion, and love. This time span opens doors to cultural expansion and avoids petty interests.

If you are busy trying to begin projects, you will not be open to receive the recognition that you have earned. You will be drawn from your neighbourhood and intimate relationships to relate to new values, cultures, and artistic trends. The balance must be maintained to sustain your own personality.

The challenge requires generosity, charity, and denial of past successes, egomania or failures. This is a time to complete actions, create priorities, and clear the decks for future growth. You may balance this challenge by understanding that you cannot conceive and deliver at the same time. Project ideals of vision. This is a challenge based upon the spirit of brotherly love, and generosity tempered with pragmatism.

CHAPTER

NUMEROLOGY COLOURS
THEIR NUMBER AND LETTER
CO-ORDINATES

COLOUR	NUMBER	LETTERS
RED	1	A, J and S
ORANGE	2	B, K and T
YELLOW	3	C, L and U
GREEN	4	D, M and V
TURQUOISE	5	E, N and W
BLUE	6	F, O and X
PURPLE	7	G, P and V
MAUVE	8	H, Q and Z
SAFFRON	9	I and R
SILVER	Spiritually Special 11	K
GOLD	Spiritually Special 22	V

November 19 1963 **Jodie Foster** (18)(9)(2)(49)(4)(30)(?)

YOUR WINNING COLOURS THAT RELATE TO NUMEROLOGY

Numbers 1 through 9 have colour co-ordinates. This system is based upon the premise that the numbers 1 through 9 are symbols that describe personality traits and experiences. Each number has co-ordinate letters. The letters in names and the letters in numbers for birth dates may be described by colours too. Colours send out vibrations that have the same meaning as their number-letter co-ordinates. Therefore, colours may be used to attract or repel specific types of personalities and activities... and Good Luck!

In the numerology system, the colour that corresponds to the vowels in a person's name are used to indicate the person's natural instincts: what they need to feel comfortable. The colour that corresponds to the consonants in a name are utilized to indicate that person's self-image and to support the first impression that they give to others.

The co-ordinate colours to the number values for all the letters in a name is worn or used for decoration to support their career talents and all areas of self expression. The colour that corresponds to the number of destiny is used to attract opportunities that fulfill that person's purpose in life.

Numerology teaches that colour co-ordinates should be used each day with a purpose in mind.

September 2 1964 **Keanu Reeves** (16) (7) (6) (31) (4) (11) (?)

TRY WEARING YOUR FIRST LETTER-FIRST NAME COLOUR

To attract comfortable relationships, people who rec-
ognise your strong point, and to attract activities that
require your approach, wear the colour that co-ordinates with the first letter of your first name. The letter
"K" should wear No. 2 and No. 11 colours. The Letter
"V" should wear No. 4 and No. 22 colours

COLOUR - NUMBER - LETTER CHART

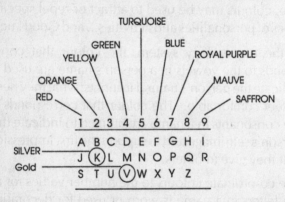

Example: DAVID - First letter 'D' = number 4 = GREEN.

All Letters:
$$4 \ 1 \ 4 \ 9 \ 4$$
$$D \ A \ V \ I \ D = 22, \ 2 + 2 = 4 = GREEN$$

Vowels: $1 \quad 9 = 10, \ 1 + 0 = 1 = RED$

Consonants $4 \quad 4 \quad 4 = 12, \ 1 + 2 - 3 = YELLOW$

November 25 1952 **Imran Khan**   (28) ① ⑦ ⑧ ㊹ ⑧ (?)

NUMBER - LETTER - COLOUR MEANINGS

1.   **RED** indicates assertiveness, creativity and ambition

2.   **ORANGE** indicates friendliness, intimacy and gentleness.

3.   **YELLOW** indicates optimism, imagination and pleasure seeking.

4.   **GREEN** indicates practicality, common sense and economy.

5.   **TURQUOISE** indicates sensuality, versatility and curiosity.

6.   **BLUE** indicates responsibility, love and parental instinct.

7.   **PURPLE** indicates aristocracy, self control and intellect.

8.   **MAUVE** indicates executive initiative, status and stamina.

9   **SAFFRON** indicates empathy, skill and quality consciousness.

11   **SILVER** indicates strong personal ideals and nervous energy.

22   **GOLD** indicates workaholic habits and nervous energy.

June 14 1969   **Steffi Graf**   (29) (2) (7) (45) (9) (20) (?)

MY LUCKY NUMBERS

	BASE NUMBER	WHEEL CHOICE 1	WHEEL CHOICE 2	WHEEL CHOICE 3	WHEEL CHOICE 4
LUCKY No. 1 My First Name Number	◯	◯	◯	◯	◯
LUCKY No. 2 My Childhood Motivation Number	◯	◯	◯	◯	◯
LUCKY No. 3 My Birthday Number	◯	◯	◯	◯	◯
LUCKY No. 4 My Destiny Number	◯	◯	◯	◯	◯
LUCKY No. 5 My Time Span Pyramid Number	◯	◯	◯	◯	◯
LUCKY NO. 6 Calendar Day Number Draw	(?)	(?)	(?)	(?)	(?)

May 31 1930   **Clint Eastwood**   (22) (4) (1) (49) (13) (18) (?)

WHAT NUMBERS WON

Week							Week						
	1	2	3	4	5	6		1	2	3	4	5	6
1							27						
2							28						
3							29						
4							30						
5							31						
6							32						
7							33						
8							34						
9							35						
10							36						
11							37						
12							38						
13							39						
14							40						
15							41						
16							42						
17							43						
18							44						
19							45						
20							46						
21							47						
22							48						
23							49						
24							50						
25							51						
26							52						

March 14 1933 *Michael Caine* (33) ⑥ ⑨ ⑮ ⑥ ⑲ ?

ELLIN DODGE

AMERICA'S LEADING
NUMEROLOGIST

Ellin Dodge, America's leading numerologist, is a noted author. Among her seven books her most popular titles include "You Are Your First Name" (1983), "You Are Your Birthday" (1985) and "Numerology Has Your Number" (1987). Books by Ellin Dodge have been sold through North America and have been translated into Spanish, Italian, Dutch and Portuguese.

In the USA, Ellin's private client list reads like a veritable Who's Who of the world of finance, international politics and culture. She consults for award winning artists, writers and entertainers, psychologists and members of the medical profession and celebrities from stage, screen and television.

Ellin plans to spread the message of Numerology to the U.K. First, "Win The Lottery!" in October 1994, as the National Lottery is launched. Her other books will be published in March/April 1995. Mail order services, including transcripts of First Name, Last Name, Destiny Profiles and Personal Prediction calendar planners will be available in 1995.